The
SOUL
in
CYBER-
SPACE

Hourglass Books are for all who long for reformation and revival within the evangelical community. As "tracts for the times" they raise major issues of the day. Each book is serious in tone and probing in style but practical rather than academic, more often a first word than the last. Designed not only to be read but discussed and acted on, Hourglass Books are for all who seek to restore the gospel to evangelicals and evangelicals to the gospel.

Books in the series:

- *Dining with the Devil: The Megachurch Movement Flirts with Modernity* by Os Guinness
- *The Evangelical Forfeit: Can We Recover?* by John Seel
- *Restoring the Good Society: A New Vision for Politics and Culture* by Don E. Eberly
- *Fit Bodies, Fat Minds: Why Evangelicals Don't Think and What to Do About It* by Os Guinness
- *Power Encounters: Reclaiming Spiritual Warfare* by David Powlison
- *Reasons of the Heart: Recovering Christian Persuasion* by William Edgar

The
SOUL
in
CYBER-
SPACE

DOUGLAS
GROOTHUIS

A Division of Baker Book House Co.
Grand Rapids, Michigan 49516

Acknowledgments

My heartfelt appreciation goes to The Trinity Forum and especially to Amy Boucher for her encouragement and dedication to this book at every stage of production. Although my wife, Rebecca Merrill Groothuis, was working hard to complete her own book, *Good News for Women*, she provided crucial editorial assistance at the eleventh hour—and before. Her wise influence touches every page. Thank you. I also thank many friends and relatives for their indispensable prayers.

To Rebecca Merrill Groothuis

who, by the grace of God,
makes me a better writer,
a better thinker,
and a better person.

CONTENTS

INTRODUCTION

CYBERSPACE AND THE TROUBLE WITH OUR SOULS

PERSONAL COMPUTER SCREENS do not usually attract a crowd, and wedding ceremonies have proceeded without the help of computers. But one couple challenged all that. Karen Bray and Keith Prior were recently married while both were in different cities. How so? They were married online, "in" cyberspace. A newspaper photo shows a small group of happy people gathered around a video monitor while a minister sitting next to the bride types in the wedding vows to be sent via e-mail.[1] If this novelty catches fire we might soon find nuptial computer programs that provide the desired sound effects, music, scenery, assorted vow possibilities (traditional, New Age, Muslim, atheist, and so on), as well as virtual ministers for the designer wedding of your choice—right in your own home, or, we should say, in cyberspace (wherever that is).

TECHNOLOGICAL ANTICIPATIONS

In today's cultural vortex of rapid technological change, half-truths and outright falsehoods swirl around us, buffeting our common sense while lifting our imaginations to new heights of revelry. Every day we hear of the promises of cyberspace, the possibilities of the Internet, and breakthroughs in all manner of computer technologies. This new medium will at once create community, break down prejudices, revolutionize business, make the world more of a global village than ever before, and possibly trigger a religious revival. Our whole manner of being will change, says computer expert Nicholas Negroponte; we must learn to orient ourselves to "being digital." In this "radically new culture" we "will socialize in digital neighborhoods in which

9

physical space will be irrelevant and time will play a different role."[2]
Those are heady words, but such talk is not uncommon when the
topic is computers.

The onset of information-expanding technologies such as radio
and television was often heralded as presaging untold blessings—
predictions we now view as naive if sincere. In 1939, David Sarnoff,
the CEO for RCA, giddily claimed that "It is probable that television
drama of high caliber and produced by first-rate artists will materially
raise the level of dramatic taste of the nation."[3] In 1997, dramatic
taste in America seems generally frozen at the level of the cartooned
imbecility of "The Simpsons," the nihilistic perversity of "Beavis and
Butthead," any number of noncartoon but cartoon-like sitcoms, "real-
ity-based" unreal simulations of the violent and indecent, image-
ruled news programs devoid of analysis and historical context, and so
forth. Media moguls regale us with promises of five hundred cable
channels' worth of the same (or worse).

Some had even higher expectations for the cathode ray tube. In
the column "Fifty Years Ago Today," the June, 1994, *Scientific American* featured this rather messianic 1944 quotation from Norman D.
Walter, president of the American Television Association:

> Television offers the soundest basis for world peace that has yet
> been presented. Peace must be created on the bulwark of under-
> standing. International television will knit together the peoples
> of the world in bonds of mutual respect; its possibilities are vast,
> indeed.[4]

Another technophile waxed messianic over a new device for
safely storing and disseminating information that could bring a "complete planetary memory for all mankind" because "the whole human
memory can be . . . made accessible to every individual." It would
not be subject to destruction because the information is not "con-
centrated in any one single place" because it "can be reproduced
exactly and fully, in Peru, China, Iceland, Central Africa, or wherever
else. . . . It can have at once the concentration of a craniate animal
and the diffused vitality of an amoebae." Moreover, "there is no practical obstacle whatever now to the creation of an efficient index to all
human knowledge, ideas, and achievements."[5] Was he speaking of
computers? No. H. G. Wells wrote these words in 1937, several

decades before the ascent of the modern computer and several more decades before anyone had heard of the Internet or the Information Superhighway. He was effusing over microfilm, which, though a helpful invention, has hardly become the intellectual elixir he envisaged.

On the one hand, technophiles dazzle us with their breathless prophecies of social regeneration through breakthrough technologies: the blind will see, the lame will walk, the poor shall thrive, and the dead shall be raised—eventually, given enough time and talent. Technological backfires—such as Chernobyl, mindless television, and computer viruses—can be overcome with enough ingenuity and fortitude. On the other hand, technophobes startle us with their pronouncements of doom: we are in a deadly duel with the technological juggernaut, whose powers ironically threaten to depersonalize and enslave the very ones who gave it birth.

TROUBLED SOULS

The soul longs to root its hope on nothing less than bedrock realities when it faces the unknowns and ordeals of social change and upheaval. After the economic exuberance of the eighties subsided, many Americans could no longer turn their backs on the social pathologies of rising crime, divorce, illegitimacy, suicide, drug abuse, abortion-on-demand, corruption, poverty, racial discord, and rampant incivility.[6] Culture-watcher William Bennett warns that *"unless these exploding social pathologies are reversed, they will lead to the decline and perhaps even to the fall of the American republic."*[7] As blood stains the streets, as lawsuits clog the courts, as popular culture rots in a stench of idiocy and perversity, many are crying out for a meaning that endures and ennobles. People thirst for a "new spirituality" to rescue them. The title of a recent *Psychology Today* article captures the mood of many: "Desperately Seeking Spirituality."[8]

These desperate cries are being answered by a raft of best-selling prescriptions for the soul, all embedded in a worldview alien to Christianity. They include *Care of the Soul* and *Soul Mates* by Jungian therapist Thomas Moore; *The Celestine Prophecy*, a New Age adventure by astrologer James Redfield; and *The Seven Spiritual Laws of Success* by Deepak Chopra, an endocrinologist who advocates the benefits of pantheistic monism—the belief that all reality is One and that all is divine. The soul has come out of the closet and "spirituality" (very broadly conceived) is all the rage.[9] Nevertheless, people remain confused and despondent. Our national character is being called into question, and integrity is ending up on the endangered species list. To multiply the confusion, a myriad of voices exclaim that our whole civilization will be radically transformed through the next phase of the computer revolution as we plunge headlong into cyberspace. Our troubled souls are headed for an exciting new territory, which is as close as our keyboards and as mysterious as the hidden hardware of our computers.

CYBERSPACE TO THE RESCUE?

Since the development and mass production of the personal computer, technological change has accelerated at an unprecedented rate, bringing transformations undreamed of only decades earlier. Computer power has been decentralized and individualized. Instead of logging on to a mainframe computer and scheduling "time sharing," individuals tap into their own computers for word-processing, game-playing, financial accounting, sending and receiving electronic mail, and any number of other functions. In this unstable but potent environment, huge computer industries have developed—and died—overnight. Microsoft has become the symbol of personal computing, with Bill Gates, its cofounder and president, the icon of the new entrepreneurism and technological optimism.

Until recently, interaction with computers was normally limited to one person working on one computer at a time. Telephones connected people by voice, but computers were solitary affairs, however riveting their powers. The concept of cyberspace has come with the development of an interactive web or network of computers. By using a modem, computers link up through phone lines to exchange data in digitized form. This network—originally engineered by the federal government for scientists to exchange research—has gone public in a big way. *Newsweek* declared 1995 "the Year of Internet."[10] What was once designed to be a military communications system built to withstand a nuclear attack has become the focus of intense public interest and discussion.[11]

The Internet is heralded as the most important cultural development of the decade, if not the century. Millions are going online each year to partake of its bounty. Netscape, an Internet browser utility, hit the stock market after one year of operation and no actual earnings with a value of more than two billion dollars, and quickly rose to six billion dollars.[12] The jazzy and off-beat magazine *Wired* has been charting the protean world of cyberspace since its first issue in 1993. Other magazines, such as *Internet Underground* and *Virtual City*, chart the cultural frontiers of cyberspace in formats that resemble Web pages more than traditional magazines (and you can be sure that the contributors list their e-mail addresses). Such movies as *Lawnmower Man, The Net,* and *Virtuosity* explore the possible social ramifications of the new technologies.

Summarizing the nature and functions of the Internet is akin to corralling a tornado. It is evolving and mutating at a brisk clip. Cyberspace covers a lot of territory—and very quickly. The Internet provides a host of services all focused on the swift and prodigious exchange of information, many of which we will visit throughout this book. This network of connections is hailed as a way for humans to extend their consciousness through rapid access to a new world of data. Our awareness itself is entering the computer networks, many claim, and may never be the same.

New "virtual communities" are developing online, as are new forms of crime, known as "hacking," where computer wizards tamper with credit ratings or even military data for fun and profit—and terror. Not content with the limitations of the Internet, Bill Gates and others hawk the benefits of the Information Superhighway, an expanded network that would unite computers, phones, televisions, and more into one system, thus providing enhanced and personalized access to a computerized ocean of data.[13] Some see it as ushering in a digitopia.

WHAT IS CYBERSPACE?

But what exactly is cyberspace? Like many pop-neologisms indiscriminately ladled out upon the bewildered, the word *cyberspace* may initially mystify more than illuminate. The prefix "cyber" is increasingly applied to almost anything. We hear of cybersex, cyberporn, cyberpunk, cybercafes, and much more. The term cyberspace was coined by science-fiction writer William Gibson in his ground-breaking novel *Neuromancer* (1984) to refer to the "space" in which computer-mediated communication occurs; that is, to the interface between digital bits and human consciousness—or between silicon and the soul. The prefix "cyber" comes from cybernetics, which is the study of self-regulating systems; it has been expanded, however, to cover all the areas where humans and computer technologies overlap in strange and stimulating ways.

For instance, a cyborg (cyber-organism) is a composite being that is part human and part computer—and one that has frequented any number of recent action-films such as "Terminator 2," which are themselves dominated by special effects generated by sophisticated computer graphics. One such effect is the animation technology of morphing, which allows identities to become fluid and indeterminate; one thing (whether person, animal, monster, or whatever) can "morph" into another and back again in a physically impossible but visually stunning and convincing manner.

Special effects and celluloid aside, the insinuation and proliferation of computers into almost every aspect of life may have transformed us all into cyborgs of one form or another. I type and retype these words by means of a word processing program; they appear and disappear on a screen; they are stored in digital form and are susceptible to all the manipulations that my computer allows—which far exceed what mere pen and paper could ever do. (Although I still scribble notes on the books and articles I read as well as on the printouts of my chapters.) I can "upload" the chapters of this book to anyone who can "download" them with a computer terminal and a modem. It makes no difference whether they live across town or in Australia, so long as they are "online."

My reflections about computers and cyberspace are (at least partially) mediated by computers and cyberspace. I am a rather pedestrian, low-tech cyborg—and, chances are, so are you—seeking to be conscious and respectful of what is distinctively human, what is dehumanizing, and how to make some sense of it all before the ethical, philosophical, and theological questions concerning the medium are absorbed by the pressing technical and political needs.

CHALLENGING THE GOD OF TECHNOLOGY

Any investigation of the fate of the soul in cyberspace must confront what social analyst Neil Postman calls "the god of Technology." This is a jealous deity who lacks official shrines, altars, tax-exempt organizations, and clergy. But it is a god, nevertheless,

> in the sense that people believe technology works, that they rely on it, that it makes promises, that they are bereft when denied access to it, that they are delighted when they are in its presence, that for most people it works in mysterious ways, that they condemn people who speak against it, that they stand in awe of it, and that, in the born-again mode, they will alter their lifestyles, their schedules, their habits, and their relationships to accommodate it.[14]

The god of Technology casts a wide and usually imperceptible net over many approaches to new technologies, directing our thoughts in predictable, if insupportable, ways. Social critic Langdon Winner laments over current "technological somnambulism." He wonders why it "is that we so willingly sleepwalk through the process of reconstituting the conditions of human existence."[15] He notes, "In the twentieth century it is usually taken for granted that the only reliable sources for improving the human condition stem from new machines, techniques and chemicals."[16] We say "Yes" to the glittering gadgets first and ask questions later: "In the technical realm we repeatedly enter into a series of social contracts, the terms of which are revealed only after signing."[17] Such seductions should be resolutely resisted in principle; sleep-walking is a disorder whenever it occurs.

The burden of this book is not to explain the intricacies of cyberspace or how to use the latest gizmos efficiently. These sorts of instruction manuals already abound (and become outdated shortly after publication). I could add nothing to them in any technical sense. Rather, I will pursue a less traveled path and address the emerging technologies of cyberspace in relation to their effects on our souls and our society. All technologies, and particularly information technologies, extensively alter our forms of life—usually in invisible or at least subtle ways. This was put baldly and uncritically at the 1933 World's Fair in Chicago. A prominent sign read, "Science explores: Technology executes: Man conforms."[18] Intentional or not, this seems to mock the theological affirmation: "Man proposes. God disposes." Technology has taken the place of deity, and people serve it instead of God.

Developing some themes from media philosopher Marshall McLuhan, Neil Postman points out that technological change is neither additive or subtractive, but ecological.[19] Removing a television from a typical teenager's room is not simply the subtraction of a piece of furniture; it alters the entire environment or ecology. The room is no longer the entertainment center it once was; books may now be retrieved from dusty shelves; conversations once muted by video may now flourish; boredom may beckon. More globally, the invention of the printing press in the fifteenth century fundamentally changed Europe, fostering increased literacy and aiding the Reformers' cause through the mass distribution of their literature.

If new technological artifacts and systems are to be challenged creatively, they must be subjected to sustained scrutiny at the early stages of their incorporation into everyday life—before they become inextricably enmeshed with other technologies and cultural practices. In order to warm up to this kind of cultural critique, we should look briefly at the effects of two ubiquitous technologies that have already become culturally entrenched, namely television and radio.

TECHNOLOGICAL EFFECTS: TELEVISION AND RADIO

Technologies tend to form interlocking systems such that an analysis of one kind of technology involves looking at several others.[20] For instance, when television became a primary means of advertising products, methods of industrial production had to alter to keep up with new demands for volume and novelty. Moreover, people's sensibilities and intellectual orientations were radically changed: the image eclipsed the word as the prevalent mode of communication, attention spans contracted in accord with the rapid pace of the fleeting video image, and a nonlinear orientation to life replaced the more orderly view of life fostered by the book.[21]

The fast-paced, image-dominated, and driven nature of television renders intellectual reflection almost impossible. Good discussion makes for bad television because the "talking head" is considered too monotonous. The silence required for cognitive comprehension is anathema on television. It cannot endure it. Time is money, and the television must fill every moment with its images and noise. Personalities encountered on screen are constructed and deconstructed through the manipulations of camera and editing. The image is everything because the essence has become unknown and unknowable.

Television also tends to drain its viewers of initiative and energy. It pacifies by its sheer power to amuse endlessly. Those conditioned by the amusement mentality become intellectually impatient and develop shortened attention spans; they also begin to expect that reality ought to be amusing. Countless hours of peering at entertaining images dulls one's apprehension of the real world and erodes the sense of community between human beings who are worthy of respect. This was tragically illustrated in the late spring of 1994 in South Philadelphia when Mohammad Jaberipour was murdered.

The forty-one-year-old father of three was working in a Mister Softee ice cream truck when he was shot after refusing to give money to a sixteen-year-old. As the man lay dying, teenagers in the area laughed and mocked him by composing a rap song for the occasion: "They killed Mr. Softee." A friend of Jaberipour, who arrived on the scene after the shooting, said, "It wasn't human. When I got there people were laughing and asking me for ice cream. I was crying. My best friend was killed. They were acting as though a cat had died, not a human being."[22] For these soulless teenagers, an agonizing, pointless death was merely a show, an opportunity to have a good time—just like on television.

Could our migration into cyberspace, with all its simulations, stimulations, and seductions, further compound this confusion of reality with a sensational media spectacle? In a less severe mode, Reva Basch, a cybarian (librarian of cyberspace), admits that her immersion in the online world tends to "have an accelerating effect on life. At parties, I'll scan the people: 'not interesting, not interesting.' Which is *awful*." She laments that she is "sort of looking over their shoulders for the next person who might *add value*."[23] Our technologies affect our ways of perceiving the rest of the world.

Radio is a technology that has been well-integrated into modern culture for decades and is almost omnipresent in developed nations. We therefore give it about as much thought as a fish does water. But in 1948, the German poet and writer Max Picard reflected on the nature of radio in his haunting work *The World of Silence*. Picard lamented the modern world's loss of silence, a silence he treasured as a positive element of God's creation and not as simply the absence of noise. "Silence belongs to the basic structure of man,"[24] he claimed; any social situation that effaces the domain of silence wounds the human soul.

Put into this framework, Picard perceived that "radio has occupied the whole space of silence. . . . Radio noise is so amorphous that it seems to have no beginning and no end; it is limitless."[25] Radio remakes people in its own image: people "become merely an appendage of the noise of the radio. Radio produces the noise and man imitates the motion of the noise."[26] In other words, we end up transmitting words that are aimed indiscriminately at others rather than engaging souls in conversation.

Radio can also break down local cultures and communities as people are absorbed into the mass, impersonal culture it creates. The introduction of the transistor radio into the traditional Lakakhi society in northwestern India led to the abandoning of communal songs in favor of canned material produced for mass distribution.[27]

Picard further observed that although radio transmits the human voice, it does so mechanically, without what he called "the proper mode of knowledge." The communion involved in reading and listening, Picard claimed, is a direct personal encounter that demands that the reader and the listener enter into the mental world of the writer or speaker. Radio, in contrast, impersonally dispenses facts "squeezed into the person listening like so much material into empty boxes."[28] Picard's conclusion is radical: "The meaning of knowledge is falsified by the radio"[29] because the irreducibly personal dimension is subverted.

> None of the elemental phenomenon of life, such as truth, loyalty, love, faith, can exist in this world of radio-noise, for these elemental phenomena are direct, clearly defined and clearly limited, original, firsthand phenomena, while the world of radio is the world of the circuitous, the involved, the indirect. In such a world the elemental phenomena are ruined.[30]

Are these merely the embittered protestations of a crusty curmudgeon? Has radio been that lethal? After all, has not the Voice of America broadcasted important truths into totalitarian nations for decades? Have not lives been saved through emergency warnings of tornadoes and hurricanes? Certainly so. Picard's lamentations may be overstated, but his primary concern should be ours as well: How does any technology alter the terms and structure of communication? Yes, radio allows information to travel much more quickly and to be distributed more broadly. This has its advantages, but the form in which the information is conveyed should be appraised as well.

If we think that listening to a sermon—even a very good sermon—on the radio is the same as joining our local congregation to be challenged by the preaching of the Word of God, we are deceived. Furthermore, if we believe that a widespread radio ministry can substitute for the dynamics of interpersonal dialogue—as we weep with those who weep and laugh with those who laugh—we are equally deceived. Such misconceptions illustrate the danger of the technological replacement of the personal. An artificial and impersonal means of communication replaces human interaction in ways that are not immediately obvious. In so doing, it debases the personal dimension that God values so highly. This dimension is simulated through radio because we hear a voice, but that voice is disembodied and randomly distributed; it is severed from its source and is not typically directed toward any person in particular.

I have emphasized the radio because, as communication technologies go, it is ancient and seems benign and beyond criticism. If we can worry this much about radio, what should we think about cyberspace? In assessing computer technologies, we should have the same concern over the technological replacement of the personal. In what ways have these technologies simulated and subverted the human element of life and other factors that we esteem as healthy for the soul?

AVOIDING WORLDLINESS

A good long squint and some head-scratching directed at the emerging world of cyberspace may equip us to make some wise choices while we yet have choices to make. From a Christian perspective, such rumination is not merely an academic exercise: It forms the heart of biblical discipleship. Followers of Christ have always lived with the creative tension of being in, but not of, the world system. They are citizens of heaven, yet emissaries of Christ on earth. As such, their pattern of life must resist the corruption and coercion of sinful ways of life in order to honor their Sovereign. As Paul warned, "Do not conform any longer to the pattern of this world, but be transformed by the renewing of your mind. Then you will be able to test and approve what God's will is—his good, pleasing, and perfect will."[31]

When worldly thought patterns prevail, forms of culture are adopted (whether knowingly or unknowingly) that are God-resisting and dehumanizing; idols are embraced instead of exposed; the relative is absolutized and the absolute relativized. Worldliness is always the enemy of Christian character and a shameful stain on the church. As Jesus said, when the salt of the earth loses its savor, it becomes good for nothing and is nothing but an embarrassment.[32]

Although the list of human vices and virtues remains constant throughout history,[33] vices cluster and contaminate specific cultures differently at different times. Worldliness takes many forms. The words of apologist and social critic Francis Schaeffer are still sobering:

> The Christian is to resist the spirit of the world. But when we say this we must understand that the world-spirit does not always take the same form. So the Christian must resist the spirit of the world *in the form it takes in his own generation.* If he does not do this he is not resisting the spirit of the world at all.[34]

It is possible to resist the vices of an earlier age—and so appear wise and righteous—while submitting to the vices of today not yet named for what they are. Our model should be the people of the Hebrew tribe of Issachar "who understood the times and knew what Israel should do."[35] Social critic Jacques Ellul issues a challenge we should heed: "The Christian has a prophetic mission to try to think before events become inevitable."[36] For, as the seventeenth-century French philosopher Blaise Pascal pointed out,

> When everything is moving at once, nothing appears to be moving, as on board ship. When everyone is moving toward depravity, no one seems to be moving, but if someone stops he shows up the others who are rushing on, by acting as a fixed point.[37]

This does not mean one must regard every new technology as the invincible advance of Antichrist or as another Tower of Babel.[38] We need not be reactionary Luddites, who want to smash new technologies simply because they alter our forms of life.[39] Human ingenuity in subduing creation, including technical facility, is part of what it means to be made in God's image.[40] Paul's imperative is apropos here as everywhere else: "Test everything. Hold on to the good. Avoid every kind of evil."[41] Nevertheless, after the testing, we will find that for the health of the soul some aspects of cyberspace need to be avoided. The Luddite impulse is not entirely off the mark.

The following chapters investigate how the technologies of cyberspace impinge on modern culture, how they shape our souls, and whether they should be received, rejected, or refined. We will specifically address the postmodern view of the self and its relation to personal identity in cyberspace; the desire of some to become disembodied and even immortal in cyberspace; the relationship of the book and the screen to the nurturance of the soul; the status of objective truth in the digital world; the burgeoning industry of cybereroticism; the new/old religion of technoshamanism, a kind of cyberanimism that finds its deities in digitality; the possibility of virtual community; and the advisability of putting Christianity online. My conclusions about the fate of the soul in cyberspace will be neither utopian nor apocalyptic, but we have some cyberspace to traverse before reaching them.

1

THE POSTMODERN
SOUL IN CYBERSPACE

OUR SOULS REFLECT OUR WORLDS and our worlds reflect our souls.
One who aspires to understand the nature of the soul ought, then, to
be an auditor of culture. The introduction of new technologies reflects
previous philosophical trends, reinforces these trends in novel ways,
and sparks the creation of new ideas and patterns of culture.
Although technologies irradiate their cultural atmospheres in
uncountable ways, the fallout is often difficult to discern unless we
endeavor to bring the background into the foreground.

WHO ARE WE?

Ironically, our very sense of ourselves, our personal identity, is formed
in an environment that is largely obscured by its very proximity and
normality. One who wears corrective lenses soon forgets their presence in going about the business of seeing. The technology becomes
invisible when it is effective; it becomes a component, an assimilated appendage or extension of the person. As Marshall McLuhan
observed, "To say that any technology or extension of man creates a
new environment is a much better way of saying that the medium
is the message. Moreover, this environment is always 'invisible.' "[1]
This new environment—involving telephone, radio, television, computer, and so on—is both the soul's reflection and its habitation.

G. K. Chesterton, the sagacious apologist of an earlier generation, mused on the mysteries of the restless soul:

> Every man has forgotten who he is. One may understand the cos-
> mos, but never the ego; the self is more distant than any star. Thou

23

shalt love the Lord thy God; but thou shalt not know thyself. We are all under the same mental calamity; we have all forgotten our names.[2]

Paradoxically, we are often very far from ourselves; just as we are very far from the most immediate and conditioning elements of our technologies, the very technologies that subtly shape and express the souls we fail to understand. Assorted sages, sorcerers, seers, and shamans have attempted to account for our existential oblivion, offering various revelations on human nature, its origin, purpose, and destiny. Scripture affirms that our disorientation indicates our fall from grace, our descent into the morass of "life under the sun" apart from God. As Pascal arrestingly, if hyperbolically, put it:

> Ecclesiastes shows that man without God is totally ignorant and inescapably unhappy, for anyone is unhappy who wills but cannot do. Now he wants to be happy and assured of some truth, and yet he is equally incapable of knowing and of not desiring to know.[3]

ASSUMED IDENTITIES

The diverse intellectual movement known as postmodernism offers us a way to live with Pascal's dilemma without ever resolving it. We simply bless the chaos, countenance the confusion, give up on knowing who we really are, and embrace a truth-less, perpetually uprooted existence. As a bumper-sticker announces, "I've given up on reality. Now I'm looking for a good fantasy." Postmodernism attempts to forge a philosophy (or an orientation) free from the need to discover natures, essences, or objective meanings. The bizarre, postmodern environment in which we live is illuminated by the following tale from cyberspace.

Author Mark Slouka tells of a friend, whom he calls Avram, who "fell in love" online.[4] This may not seem too strange, since many romances have been initiated and cultivated through letters and phone calls. Why not find love in cyberspace? The plot thickens, however—as does the perversity. Avram was an on-going participant in a MOO, a virtual world (having nothing to do with cows) that is a particular type of MUD.[5] If you are still confused, a MUD is a multiuser dialogue or dimension or dungeon, depending on whom you talk to. Participants, called users, interact by posting messages according to the ambiance agreed upon for the environment. MOOs are all fantasy worlds in one sense or another, being rooted in fantasy role-playing games such as the occult Dungeons and Dragons.

These games have no official winners or losers or hard rules; rather, they are artificial cultures in which users adopt various identities in relationship to other assumed identities, whether wizards, witches, gods, goddesses, angels, demons, extraterrestrials, or more pedestrian personae. Players interact in larger groups or become more involved through private "rooms" (or dialogue boxes) in which others are excluded. Some of these environments, variously customized for differing tastes, use avatars or graphical figures that can be manipulated in various ways to gesture and speak in a caption. The technologies are somewhat rudimentary, but are likely to advance quickly.[6] Sherry Turkle, a psychologist and philosopher of cyberspace, claims that there are over five hundred of these virtual worlds, populated by hundreds of thousands of virtual people, most in their twenties and thirties.[7]

Avram, a graduate student in political science, a husband and a father, was infatuated with a MOO where he assumed the identity of "Allison." Avram allowed Slouka to join his MOO and interact for a few moments with "Janine," a long-term friend of Allison's. Janine related that she had met the "love of her life" online, whom she contacted every day. Slouka asked if it was difficult to move from VR (virtual or computer-generated reality) to RL (real life). The answer: "We've never met in RL (sigh!). . . . I don't expect we ever will. It would be too hard." At this, Avram became distraught and took back the keyboard from Slouka.

Later Avram confessed to Slouka that he (as Allison) had been having an online affair with Janine. They had met in VR five times a week for two years. Avram, then, was a man pretending to be a woman who was in love with a woman who thought Avram was a woman. For Janine the affair was lesbian; but not for Avram. They had even "had sex" in VR—"sex" without contiguity, without physicality, without honesty, without matrimony, and without fixed identity. (We will attempt a prudent discussion of virtual sex in chapter six.) Avram would not drop his online identity as Allison and he would not forsake Janine. What about Avram's real-life wife? She knew nothing of it; although Avram would, according to Slouka, periodically "space out for five or ten minutes at a time . . . because he wasn't here, in his actual living room, say, but rather with Janine, in cyberspace."[8]

Avram was "spacing out" not only for five or ten minutes at a shot, but for hours on end while connecting with Janine—who, for all we know, might be a man pretending to be a woman, which, many think, happens far more frequently than the opposite. Avram had constructed an artificial identity that took on a life of its own, a virtual life so insistent and addictive that it overwhelmed his life outside cyberspace. Slouka notes that this online affair had become irreversible. Avram expected that he and Janine would continue this illicit online impersonation "for the rest of their lives, or until that day when one of them failed to log on."[9] Even if the liaison ended, Allison would remain a part of Avram's identity. To destroy her would be to kill his persona. The virtual Allison had taken up residence in the real Avram, thus destabilizing his real-life family—although Slouka claims Avram was "secure in his sexual identity,"[10] at least offline.

What does this account of assumed identities have to do with postmodernism? The strange yarn about Allison and Janine illustrates and reinforces a postmodernist theme. Taking on various identities in varying circumstances is sanctioned by this new movement, for it exemplifies the death of belief in the unitary self, the hard ego, the irreducible center of personal identify. Identity is not fixed, but fluid; not singular, but multiple; not prescribed, but protean; not defined, but diffused. Psychologist Kenneth Gergen rejoices in the replacement of the one person with a multitude of personae: "The mask may not be the symbol of superficiality that we have thought it was, but the means of realizing our potential." He then adverts to poet Walt Whitman's anomalous affirmation: "Do I contradict myself? Very well, then, I contradict myself. (I am large. I contain multitudes.)"[11]

The accusation of being "double-minded" or "duplicitous"—as when the Apostle James cautions us not to be double-minded and thus unstable in all our ways[12]—may no longer be taken as an insult. Rather it is seen as part of being a walking, talking multitude of contradictions. Better, even, to be triple-minded, or quadruple-minded, or just plain many-minded. Just as postmodernism rejects monotheism as an illegitimate attempt to monopolize the deity, so too it rejects the individual self as an illegitimate attempt to straightjacket psychology. The result? We have internalized the sociological pluralism of our culture as a psychological plurality of selves.

In some ways, Western individualism, with its strong sense of the autonomous self, may be splintering by reason of its own insufficiency. As modern individualism developed out of the Enlightenment, it severed the self from its Source, releasing it to realize its own potentials unfettered by any outside authority. This modernist self has attempted to integrate its desires, values, and beliefs into a consistent whole without a theological authority or orientation.[13] The Christian notion of the self, in contrast, is rooted in the biblical doctrine of our creation in the image and likeness of God and our possession of an immaterial soul with its own distinctive attributes that persists over time.

Many contemporary critics are pronouncing the death of the solid self and are announcing the birth of the decentered and diffused self, which floats on the shifting surface of our pluralistic culture. In a militantly anti-existentialist pronouncement, the French postmodernist philosopher and psychologist Jacques Lacan stated, "I am not a poet. I am a poem." The self today is more of a passive medium for a host of cultural forces than a fundamental center of meaning and value; it has become an assemblage of diverse and even contradictory aspects that lack coherence and objective significance. Both world and soul are thus chaotically kaleidoscopic—without anchor, without center, and without circumference. Meanings are not discovered or even invented, but are toyed with and sampled for a variety of purposes. Fictions cannot be exposed, unmasked, or refuted by realities; fictions are all we have left, and fictions are what we are. Of course, when the self traffics in nothing but fictions, the notion of truth as nourishment for the soul slips from our grasp.

FRAGMENTATION, NOT ALIENATION

This is why journalist Benjamin Woolley observes that "artificial reality is the authentic postmodern condition, and virtual reality its definitive technological expression."[14] Virtual reality, in a general sense, is the simulated environment generated by computer graphics in which one can become immersed to various degrees. The statement that "the artificial is the authentic" may ring oxymoronic to many, yet this is the postmodern posture, however dizzying. Turkle notes that the postmodern self is not alienated, but fragmented. Alienation assumes the existence of a centered and singular self that has become lost or obscured. The alienated self is separated from itself. But if the self is not a singular entity to begin with, there is nothing from which it can be alienated. (Supposedly, the idea of a real self occurs only when one falsely attaches enduring and constituting attributes to oneself in a process of reifying the artificial.) The postmodern self suffers from an "anxiety of identity," yet without estrangement from its true identity, since that fails to exist at all.[15]

This sense of dislocation without hope of homecoming tends to be perpetuated by the sensibilities and structures of cyberspace. Turkle contends that certain postmodernist ideas are fostered by computer technologies, causing these ideas to be appropriated by many who will never crack a book by postmodernist philosophers Lacan, Derrida, or Foucault. Someone may purchase a computer for reasons of efficiency or social status without realizing that "the medium is the message," that this particular extension of human endeavor is not neutral: it carries with it a propensity toward certain perspectives and experiences. When people enter cyberspace they may play multiple roles and possibly play characters of the opposite sex. "In this way," Turkle observes, "they are swept up by experiences that enable them to explore previously unexamined aspects of their sexuality or that challenge their ideas about a unitary self."[16]

The phrase "swept up" is the one to highlight. When we become engrossed in the capacities of a powerful new technology, our critical faculties may be overwhelmed by the pragmatics of making the thing work and by the sheer sensory delight of exploring new experiences. The thrill of driving a sports car for the first time might override our normal concerns with safety on the road. The power under the hood may lure us to indulge personality traits we normally keep in check or never knew existed. Speed may later become habitual. Similarly, and more subtly, the strange powers of cyberspace may draw out our responses in unpredictable and almost undetectable ways.

The fantasy enclaves discussed above allow for the adoption of any number of self-constructed identities that exhibit various components of one's self (however perversely). These identities leave behind all the richness of physical presence and embodied communication, as we will explore in the next chapter. Instead, they are textual (and sometimes graphical) splinters of personalities projected at lightning speed from keyboards to screens and back again. A man who would never consider being a cross-dresser in real life may be tempted to "gender surf" on the Net. The risk of exposure is unlikely, the commitment to the assumed identity is low (at least initially— remember Allison), and the experiences are easily available—all without having to learn how to apply mascara or navigate with heels. One may put on and take off identities because the means for doing so are so readily at hand. The mouse awaits your directions—and no one has to know (besides God).

Although he does not discuss computer-mediated identities, Thomas Moore adopts an essentially polytheistic psychology of the self. In *Care of the Soul* (1992) he claims that monotheistic faith— belief in one personal God—restricts the possibilities of the self.[17] Any belief that demands we restrict our allegiance to some objective truth is deemed cramped and unhealthy for the soul, because such views inhibit further growth and inner exploration.[18] To cultivate the soul one must realize and explore its polymorphous potential; there are many layers, many selves, many deities, many myths by which to live, none of which are morally binding on all people. This inner-worldly polytheism replaces the overt animism of tribal cultures while incorporating many of their myths, legends, and sacred ceremonies in a psychologized forum. The deities found within are allowed to express their archetypal powers unhindered by any monotheistic moralizing about idols. For Moore and his cohorts, the self is decentered and remythologized—as well as opened to occult practices, which he claims serve as tools for self-discovery.

This endorsement of a decentered self and experimentation with a new polytheism reveals that many souls have given up on finding any unified and comprehensive worldview. When God, as the source and center of ultimate meaning, value, and significance, evaporates from the social scene, a bevy of busy idols rushes in to stake out the vacant territory. When the transcendence of God is rejected, the meaning of personhood is annulled; for persons are cut off from the only reference point that explains their origin, nature, purpose, and destiny. Without anchorage beyond itself, the self floats on the waves of instability and attempts to find peace by affirming its random multiplicities and uncertainties. As sociologist Peter Berger astutely notes,

Dostoyevsky's dictum that "if God does not exist, everything is permitted" also implies that "any self is possible—and the question as to which of the many possible selves is 'true' becomes meaningless" because the self dissolves into its socializations.[19]

THE DISSOLVING SELF AND ITS DISCONTENTS

The dissolving self is deemed as natural in our postmodern world, where the fixed point of spiritual and moral authority is receding to the vanishing point. As Pascal astutely observed:

> Those who lead disorderly lives tell those who are normal that it is they who deviate from nature, and think they are following nature themselves; just as those who are on board ship think that the people on shore are moving away. Language is the same everywhere: we need a fixed point to judge it. The harbour is the judge of those aboard ship, but where are we going to find a harbour in morals?[20]

The disorder of the decentered self is felt even by Sherry Turkle, who brings a postmodernist philosophy to her analysis of cyberspace. In an interview in *Wired* magazine she affirms, "The goal of healthy personality development is not to become a One, not to become a unitary core, it's to have a flexible ability to negotiate the many— [to] cycle through multiple identities." We need to "have access to many aspects of the self" and "to negotiate, to fit them together in some way."[21] The interviewer agreed with Turkle's view but asked her about the notion of "authenticity," which gave Turkle some pause. She admitted that she "worked very hard to establish a stable, coherent, authorial voice" in her book *Life on the Screen*. "And in a way that's at odds with my message about postmodernism. Or is it?"[22] Turkle ponders, "We are both single and multiple voices. I'm struggling with this issue; many others are too. It's central to me." She admits that "people have strong feelings of needing something unitary."[23]

Turkle struggles to find meaning in a self that is diffused, decentered, and dissolved in cyberspace. She lacks, as do many other cyberspace citizens, "a fixed point," as Pascal says, from which to know and orient herself in her world, whether in cyberspace or elsewhere. Lacking the concept of the human fall from grace,[24] Turkle can only attempt to justify the fragmentation of the self that is evidenced and amplified by the artificial identities donned in cyberspace. Yet she still senses the need for something more, some way of binding oneself to a coherent identity. The celebration of multiple selves really stems from the bankruptcy of any one self to handle all of life's complexities and challenges. Multiplicity is hallowed by default. One inadequate self shattered into a dozen pieces, however, holds little promise to deliver a well-integrated life. It is Humpty-Dumpty revisited.

The same need for reality is expressed by philosopher Michael Heim in a book exploring the nature of cyberspace. He writes candidly:

> We cannot locate the anchor for our reality check outside this fluctuating, changing world. No universal divinity ensures an invariant stability for things. But we need some sense of metaphysical anchoring, I think, to enhance virtual worlds. A virtual world can be virtual only as long as we can contrast it with the real (anchored) world.[25]

This question of ultimate reality cries out for attention, but Heim begs the question concerning God's existence and opts instead for Taoism, a worldview lacking a transcendent and personal God who speaks to us. The *Tao Te Ching*, the primary text of Taoism, famously denies any word from beyond ourselves: "The Tao [Way] that can be told of is not the eternal Tao. The name that can be named is not the eternal name."[26] A nameless silence has nothing to utter about the soul's realities.

Heim and Turkle are straining to find the authentic and authoritative, the final word on self and morals, in a wild and pluralistic postmodern situation. If Turkle had written her study of cyberspace according to the philosophy she espouses, it would have been more of a compendium of incoherent remarks than a continuity of thought. Books of this irrational ilk are increasingly available, to be sure, but Turkle is too much of a bona fide philosopher to indulge this dissonance.

Turkle's troubled ruminations on the nature of the self disclose a disorientation and fragmentation in the human condition long lamented by philosophers, poets, prophets, and theologians. Although we all possess an identity that differentiates us from others, the core of which we deem to be our souls, we are, ironically, not naturally at home with ourselves. Those who claim that we possess many selves, or that we simply are many selves in some fundamental way, inherit the problem of identifying who or what chooses and wears the selves in question. People do adjust their behaviors to their situations and are affected by peer pressure; this is hardly a revelation.[27] But unless we presuppose a personal agent, a unitary doer, at the center of the various behaviors, we cannot conserve the ideas of rational choice and moral accountability. A cluster of selves will not suffice as a livable model of the person.

THE SELF IN CHRISTIAN PERSPECTIVE

A self with diverse and confusing tendencies, however, has been the human lot—east of Eden. Philosopher William James observed that all religions, despite their titanic differences in worldview, affirm that something is wrong with humans that needs to be corrected.[28] As Chesterton put it, "The primary paradox of Christianity is that the ordinary condition of man is not his sane or sensible condition; that the normal itself is an abnormality."[29] The Christian faith explains our homelessness, fragmentation, and abnormality as the result of being estranged from our Creator, a condition we both inherit from our original parents and indulge through the misuse of our moral responsibility. Our alienation extends to our relationships with others, with nature, and with our very selves. Pascal describes the human fall into sin, speaking from God's perspective,

> He wanted to make himself his own centre and do without my help. He withdrew himself from my rule, setting himself up as my equal in his desire to find happiness in himself, and I abandoned him to himself.[30]

Being abandoned to ourselves, making ourselves our own center, paradoxically produces a decentered and disoriented self—entranced by its own diversity yet troubled by its own divisiveness. One who plays a variety of roles online may enjoy expressing the varied elements of oneself, but which elements are true and good? Which should be banished or marginalized? Which should be honored and encouraged? Kenneth Gergen attacks "the code of coherence, which demands we ask, 'How can I be X if I am really Y, its opposite?' Instead, we should simply try to discern, 'What is causing me to be X at this time?' " Although we should be "concerned with tendencies that disrupt our preferred modes of living and loving . . . we should not be anxious, depressed or disgusted when we find a multitude of interests, potentials and selves."[31] But anxiety is the natural result when we lack the criteria by which to rank our tendencies, order our impulses, restrain evil, and exalt and establish the good. Cyberspace itself is resoundingly mute on these queries. It may provide a medium for the varied expressions of the manifold self, but it cannot help unify the multitude, convert the cacophony into a choir, or bring solace to the soul. When used as a theater of assumed identities, it may do just the opposite.

The purported value of the decentered self has been oversold and its detriments underrated. Even in the postmodern world, people tend to praise those who are well-balanced, who have integrity, who hate hypocrisy and are reliable because their characters are well-formed and knowable. Integrity is still saluted and desired. Those whom we regard as heroes demonstrate a strength of character that endures and prevails over adversity. The decentered self, however, self-destructs on all counts. When we describe someone as "spineless" or "like a chameleon," these are not accolades. If we claim that a politician has been "all over the map" on a particular issue, we are impugning his character in light of his inconsistency. Any appeal to a "decentered self" or a "diffused sense of identity" simply will not excuse ethical inconsistencies, online or off.

A SELF FOR ALL SEASONS

The Christian worldview provides a philosophical basis for the idea of a unitary self, explains the self's dissolute drives, and offers hope for a consolidation and amplification of the good in the soul through the healing and redemption offered by God in Christ. Let us touch briefly on these classical Christian themes in relation to the multiple identities available in cyberspace.

All of us partake of a human nature or essence that allows us to have knowledge of God and separates us from the animal kingdom. Being created in the image and likeness of God, we reflect God's personality, moral agency, and intelligence in derivative and finite ways. This grounds our identity in our Creator, not in chance natural forces nor solely in our surroundings. As Berger notes, "If there is a true self, it can only be revealed as true in a transcendent frame of reference."[32]

Despite our fallenness, human nature still reflects something of God—however distorted and fragmented that reflection may be. This disturbing distortion need not be terminal. Human nature can be restored through the life, death, and resurrection of the mediator between God and humans, Jesus Christ.[33] Through faith, erring mortals can find perfect acceptance with the Author of life, overcome fragmentation, and focus their personalities in service of Christ and his kingdom. This can be seen in several ways.

Through trusting the biblical record as God's instructions for his creatures and by being open to the leading of the Holy Spirit, we can identify which aspects of ourselves should be cultivated and which should be extinguished or reformed. The glory of the gospel allows us to recognize ourselves for who we truly are: morally corrupt beings in desperate need of a grace outside ourselves, a grace received by Christ's sacrificial death on the cross.[34] Jesus, whose death and resurrection are sufficient to render us righteous before God, also challenges us to unify and thus harness our personalities under his lordship.

Living under the lordship of Christ will mean the death of some possible selves—immoral selves dominated by lust, theft, murder, adultery, greed, malice, deceit, lewdness, envy, slander, arrogance and folly.[35] Yet, we—and everyone around us—are far better off for their demise. The psalmist prayed for a unified soul before the one true God: "Teach me your way, O LORD, and I will walk in your truth; give me an undivided heart, that I may fear your name."[36] The gospel offers us a self centered on Christ, a self sufficient for all seasons.

Jesus Christ embodied an integrated, focused, and supremely meaningful life that serves as our undying pattern for discipleship. Jesus, as the perfect human, obeyed the will of his heavenly Father, was empowered by the Holy Spirit, and lived in accord with God's written revelation. He endured and overcame temptation, avoided distractions that would have dissipated his energies, and incarnated not only deity but sinless humanity and absolute integrity. Even more, Christ transforms his people to be like him.

The Apostle Paul emphasizes the way of the soul's liberation through the power of Christ in the Holy Spirit. Life in the presence and animation of the Spirit bears the lasting fruit of "love, joy, peace, patience, kindness, goodness, faithfulness, gentleness and self-control."[37] Outside the Spirit's control lie the "acts of the sinful nature," which are "sexual immorality, impurity and debauchery; idolatry and witchcraft; hatred, discord, jealously, fits of rage, selfish ambition, dissensions, factions and envy, drunkenness, orgies, and the like."[38]

Besides the fruit of the spirit, Paul also speaks of the diverse gifts of the Spirit given for the building up of the church and the evangelizing of the world. While all disciples of Jesus are called to exhibit the fruit of the Spirit, the respective gifts are distributed as the Spirit wills to different people.[39] Finding our spiritual gifts liberates us from the need to emulate what is impossible for us and allows us to channel our energies into the abilities God has given us. Our calling in Christ combines what we love to do with what we excel in doing and what needs to be done for the glorification of God, the edification of the church, and the good of the world. As Frederick Buechner put it, "The place God calls you to is the place where your deep gladness and the world's deep hunger meet."[40]

For those souls not firmly anchored in Christ's salvation and commission, cyberspace can be hazardous to virtue and the human flourishing that God intends. The sometimes intensive interaction occurring in chat rooms, MOOs, MUDs, and other forums is largely anonymous and can easily be contrived. Furthermore, as we have seen, it can become addictive and destructive as aspects of the self are split off and take on a bizarre life of their own.

Nevertheless, some are heralding cyberspace as a means to release the soul from the prison of the body. They hail the digital age as ushering in a new era of disembodied intelligence that is free to explore and inhabit an electronic realm of almost infinite possibilities. Are they right?

2

DISEMBODIED EXISTENCE IN A DIGITAL WORLD

MUCH OF HUMAN ENDEAVOR has been concerned with how to throw off the limitations of our mortal bodies. Many ancient religious traditions teach that the soul's final salvation is available only in a permanently disembodied state. The immortality of the soul and its superiority to the physical body have been a staple of Greek philosophies such as Platonism and Neoplatonism, and of non-Semitic religions such as Gnosticism, Hinduism, Buddhism, and many of the New Age expressions today. The recent fascination with angels lies largely in their immateriality, their spiritual abilities to influence the material world without being limited to it.[1] The vicissitudes of the body—its ongoing hunger for scarce resources, its unhappy enslavement to entropy, its susceptibility to pain, its resolute disobedience to the will and the imagination—have caused many to ban it from the realm of final redemption. If we are to be saved at all, we must be saved *from* the body, not *in* it. In the end, matter does not matter; it is best forgotten. Creation, incarnation, and resurrection are alien categories in this spiritual scheme. Disincarnation is the final prize, for creation was either a mistake or an illusion.

TECHNOLOGICAL ESCAPE FROM THE BODY

The urge to transcend the impediments of the corporeal cosmos is not limited to overtly religious expressions. Much of the technological imperative finds its restless energy in the desire to lessen or eliminate the agonies of embodied existence in a world so resistant to the yearnings of the soul. We think of "labor-saving devices" such as dish-

37

washers, washing machines, or power lawn movers as augmenting our productive powers while diminishing our physical efforts. Modern medicine, at its best, strives to preserve and protect the human body from disease and decay through a host of diagnostic, chemical, and interventive technologies. Communications technologies such as the telegraph, telephone, microphone, radio, and television extend the range of our words and compensate for our limitations.

Cyberspace offers its own kind of disembodiment. As we have said, cyberspace is a region or zone where information is deposited, exchanged, and retrieved by means of data-bits that are microscopically inscribed in silicon and then, via computer systems, zip through the telephone wires from screen to screen. How can silicon become a medium for the disembodied soul? What promise, if any, does cyberspace hold for our emancipation from matter? A look at older technologies will help us answer this question, for disembodiment as an effect of technology is nothing new.

Information technologies disembody the information they carry to various degrees. Even the shift from an oral to a written culture tended to disembody knowledge. What once required memorization and recitation by living persons could now be retrieved through the dead pages of papyri, parchment, or paper. The books themselves, however, were material objects bearing the intellectual marks of their authors. They were read, handled, annotated, and distributed by persons. (I will have more to say on this in the next chapter.)

Or take the telephone. It extends the voice far beyond the capacities of the vocal chords but also severs the voice from the face and body. Early users of the telephone found such a visually diminished exchange awkward and artificial. But, of course, they adapted and forgot the initial strangeness. Philosopher Albert Borgman explores the interpersonal transformations wrought by the telephone.

> Telephoning has . . . diminished the visits that bring us fully and really face to face with one another. To a visitor we perforce disclose our entire being such as it is here and now, in the sadness of our facial expression perhaps, the slump in our posture, the carelessness of our clothing, the disarray of our dwelling. But having so revealed ourselves, we can also hope for real consolation—a concerned look, a reassuring hand from someone who will clean up the table, wash the dishes, and fix the chair.[2]

Telephonic communication, for all its benefits, isolates the voice from the body and the fuller shared environment and so crimps the nuance, subtlety, and serendipity incarnated in another's physical presence. Telephone networks aspire toward an electronic ubiquity, but they do so at the expense of eliminating or at least diminishing the place of touch, sight, and smell. As Borgman observes, "If everyone is indifferently present regardless of where one is located on the globe, no one is commandingly present." They have a "diminished presence, since we can always make them vanish if their presence becomes burdensome," or we can screen them out (as with answering machines and voice mail).[3] It is also far easier to "hang up" on someone than to spurn them face-to-face.

Of course, if a connection by telephone is the only communication link at hand, it can be a boon to the soul. While in Russia a few years ago, I called my wife Becky in Colorado to find that she had just bought a house in our new home city of Denver. The instant accessibility of the information and the impossibility of a more personal contact made the phone call a gift. Similarly, I have prayed with people over the phone when that was the only thing available to us. Nevertheless, the technology may become invisible, habitual, and anesthetizing—and so eliminate the richer dimensions accessible in face-to-face communication.

As with the telephone, we know when we listen to the radio that there is a body projecting the voice, but it is opaque to us. Hypocrisy comes more easily and deception is more efficient. ("Was that the president I heard or someone impersonating him?") Furthermore, the voice is not directed to nor does it interact with a particular person; rather, it is broadcast to a largely unknown and unknowable "audience." Again, we approach ubiquity at the price of presence; the voice extends as the person recedes.

DISEMBODIMENT, CYBERSPACE-STYLE

Many of the burgeoning technologies of cyberspace promise a similar emancipation from the drag of the body, but ironically so. The very material world that so hampers the insatiable desires of the soul provides the wherewithal for the technologies that aim to release the body from its captivity. A host of cyberphilosophers exhibit an almost Gnostic approach to matter while simultaneously worshiping the ability of material technologies to provide them with the medium for their disembodiment. The pretechnological Gnostics sought to untangle the soul from its "enmeshment" in matter. Cyber-Gnostics, however, have struck a bargain with the underachieving earth. Instead of rejecting it as pure refuse, they use its physical resources as the launching pad into an artificial, but strangely spiritual, realm of being. The soul may find new freedoms in cyberspace. But how?

The self seems especially protean and plastic when largely removed from the envelopments of real-life interaction with other human beings. It may feel more free. A newspaper article called "Health on the 'Net: A place to flee from phobias" tells of a woman suffering from a manic depression that resulted in extreme anxiety in social situations, largely isolating her in her home. Going online, however, gave her a way to communicate freely with those otherwise removed from her. Through a list-serve group called Walkers in Darkness, she connected with others with the same problem. (A list-server allows users to send messages on particular topics that are then automatically sent to people with the same interests who can respond in turn.) She comments that when online "you are only known by what you write, and not how you look or how you come across in person." She also said that a physical support group can be threatening, with its expectation that one will contribute something. "Not so on e-mail. Anonymity is very comforting. And one can leave as quietly as they joined, with no fanfare."[4] The glow of letters on the screen did not bring the terror of a person's gaze.

Has this woman found freedom? Yes and no. Yes, in that she can communicate more broadly than before. Her words can be transmitted to others who in turn can reply, from screen to screen on their own terms. But no, because her freedom comes at the cost of never experiencing embodied presence within the psychology, geography, and architecture of civilized life. If the woman were incorrigibly manic-depressive, we might rejoice in her meager technological compensations. At least she can now express her personality through writing and receiving messages on the screen—and possibly obtain some help. Nevertheless, the comforts of the inert screen as opposed to the corporeal contingencies of common life may serve to reinforce her fear of public situations, further isolating and insulating her from living presences.

Moreover, the advice she receives may be cloaked in anonymity, thus obscuring the credentials of those advising her. Constance Dalberg, a psychologist who frequently monitors various medical "newsgroups" (or list-servers), notes that in the thirty-nine newsgroups she has monitored "most individuals do not post [messages] in a way that allows their credentials to be obvious." The credentials may also be ambiguous, as when someone identifies himself as "Dr." Somebody, even when the doctorate may be in a nonmedical field.[5] Given the nature of such communication, outright deception cannot be ruled out either. A masquerade would be easier to execute in the recesses of cyberspace than in face-to-face conversation.

The mentally ill are not the only ones who may want to escape the sloppy and unpredictable environments of the natural, material world. As social critic William Irwin Thompson has observed, many Americans are less concerned to augment or correct nature than to replace it with technologies that can be programmed to obey.[6] Disneyland is better than what it simulates because it is safe, sanitized, and full of youthful employees with perpetual smiles.[7] The same dynamic is at work in cyberspace. One need not trek to public library when all the needed resources are online and as close as the keyboard. A new universe awaits.

Ken Karakotsios, formerly employed by Apple Computer, designed a computer program to simulate the supposed evolution of life, called SimLife, in which "you create a hyperlife world and set loose little creatures into it to coevolve into a complexifying artificial ecology." Karakotsios is now endeavoring to "write the biggest and best game of life, an ultimate living program." But he admits, "You know, the universe is the only thing big enough to run the ultimate game of life. The only thing wrong with the universe as a platform is that it is currently running someone else's program."[8] Karakotsios appears to recognize the evidence for intelligent design (or a "programmer") in the universe,[9] yet he wants to improve on it by creating his own cyberlife, a designer-reality free from the glitches of the unwired world. To reverse the biblical statement, what is impossible with God is possible with programmers.[10]

ENTERING CYBERSPACE?

The fantasy of actually entering cyberspace was the theme of two recent movies, *Lawnmower Man* and *Lawnmower Man, II*. In the first installment, the protagonist, Jobe, first experiences cyberspace through suiting up for virtual reality; then in a later scene he declares, "I'm going to . . . complete the final stage of my evolution. I'm going to project myself into the mainframe computer; I'll become pure energy."[11] Of course, the energy of circuitry is not pure in the sense of being natural or inexhaustible or impregnable, but Jobe's quest for disembodied transcendence is in full view, nevertheless.

In a similar vein, William Gibson's founding cyberpunk novel *Neuromancer* (1984) calls the body "wetware" and the embodied world "meatspace." In it Gibson describes a computer addict who laments losing his ability to load his consciousness into the computer matrix.

> For Case, who'd lived for the bodiless exultation of cyberspace, it was the Fall. In the bars he'd frequented as a cowboy hotshot, the elite stance involved a certain relaxed contempt for the flesh. The body was meat. Case fell into the prison of his own flesh.[12]

Even outside of science-fiction entertainment, some harbor the desire to throw off the meat and head for the silicon. Hans Moravec, the director of the Mobile Robot Laboratory in Carnegie-Mellon's Field Robotics Center, has made an ersatz religion out of robotics. Not one to restrain technological optimism, Moravec claims in his *Mind Children: The Future of Robot and Human Intelligence*, "I believe that robots with human intelligence will be common within fifty years." He does admit, though, that "by comparison, the best of today's machines have minds more like those of insects than humans."[13] This statement assumes that human intelligence is nothing more than highly sophisticated computation carried out by what scientist Marvin Minksy once called "meat machines."[14] While older materialists such as Bertrand Russell believed that their worldview doomed them to extinction, Moravec claims that immortality is achievable—with a little robotic assistance, that is.

In a dramatic narration, Moravec describes a scene where you are wheeled into a robotic operating room where your skull is anesthetized. As you remain fully conscious, the robot–surgeon opens the brain case and scans your brain for all relevant data, which is recorded in a computer. After elaborately describing the details of this process, he continues:

Layer after layer of the brain is simulated, then excavated. Eventually your skull is empty, and the [robotic] surgeon's hand rests deep in your brainstem. Though you have not lost consciousness, or even your train of thought, your mind has been removed from the brain and transferred to a machine. In a final, disorienting step the surgeon lifts out his hand. Your suddenly abandoned body goes into spasms and dies. For a moment you experience only quiet and dark. Then, once again, you can open your eyes. Your perspective has shifted. The computer simulation has been disconnected from the cable leading to the surgeon's hand and reconnected to a shiny new body of the style, color, and material of your choice. Your metamorphosis is complete.[15]

The original fragile housing for the brain is discarded as an evolutionary vestige—fit for a museum, maybe, but not for a brain. Your consciousness, nevertheless, can live forever, since duplicate copies of your mind can be made when the machinery storing it wears out.[16] You may even be beamed by laser into robots on other planets.[17] Moravec's book can be found in the nonfiction section of the library and bookstore.

A group of maverick technophiles called Extropians (from extropy, the opposite of entropy) have seized these digitopian scenarios and have become, in social critic Mark Dery's words, "cyberculture's most vocal proponents of consigning the body to the scrap heap of the twentieth century."[18] Their philosophy, not lacking in optimism, is also known as transhumanism: humanity may be transcended through future technologies that overcome entropy and death itself. To believe otherwise, according to them, is to be a "deathist."

Extropian David Ross says that because brain structure is nothing more than the hard wiring, we ought to aspire to discard the body and upload the mind into "the world-wide Cyberspace Web."[19] This brand of technovitalism draws inspiration from the egoism of Ayn Rand and the will-to-power pronouncements of Friedrich Nietzsche. Dery's description of this group as "the human potential movement on steroids" is apt.[20] Their alchemy does not seek to turn base metals into gold, but flesh into silicon and consciousness into bits—cyberworld without end, amen.[21]

The quintessential error of those hoping for a digital immortality is their confusion of the material brain with the immaterial mind.

They reduce all mental activity—intending, hoping, willing, rejoicing, lamenting, loving—to nothing but the arrangement of meat. But, as philosophers have long argued, this confuses the subjective consciousness with the objective organism. Brain states accompany mental states in our physical bodies, but they cannot be proven to be identical to them without remainder. My thought of a pink elephant does not correspond to any verifiable pink elephant image in my gray matter. As Chesterton deftly put it:

> It is obvious that a materialist is always a mystic. It is equally true that he is often a mystagogue. He is a mystic because he deals entirely in mysteries, in things that our reason cannot picture; such as mindless order or objective matter merely becoming subjective mind.[22]

The most sophisticated computer is still a machine that computes data; it knows nothing of meaning; it has no insight; it gives no wisdom.[23] Insight and wisdom concerning meaning and truth are reserved for persons with souls. Because of this fundamental distinction between mind and matter, the hope of sending a digitized consciousness into cyberspace is nothing more than a pipe dream, however elaborately envisioned or breathlessly intoned.[24]

It is quite a ride from talking on the telephone to uploading consciousness and dispensing with the body, but with each step the human body and the material creation at large are put into a new perspective generated by technological innovations (or the hope thereof, in the case of Extropians and Moravec). C. S. Lewis's prediction of a "Materialist Magician," voiced through the hopeful demon Screwtape, seems to find its fulfillment in the dreams of cyberspace. Screwtape exults: "If once we can produce our perfect work . . . the man, not using, but veritably worshipping, what he vaguely calls 'Forces' while denying the existence of 'spirits'—then the end of the war will be in sight."[25] The "Forces" of unbounded circuitry that carry cybernauts into the land of digital omniscience and immortality is not far from Screwtape's dreams, however far it is from reality.

THE BIBLICAL VIEW OF THE PHYSICAL WORLD

We may dismiss the more extreme speculations of digital resurrection as mere digitopianism. Nevertheless, these farfetched notions highlight an orientation to the physical world that opposes the Christian doctrines of creation, humanity, and God himself. When God is removed from one's worldview, such speculations, however desperate and illogical, become the only hope for surviving the death of the body.

Critics of the new digital disembodiment, such as Mark Dery and Mark Slouka, have interpreted the flight from the flesh as an outworking of an essentially Christian hatred of the body. If so, the cyberians are simply attempting to use technology to accomplish the immortality that the faithful have left to God.

Slouka claims that the talk of digital immortality and freedom from the body are rooted in "a rather unoriginal techno-Christianity," which is "hostile to the body" and yearns for another world superior to this one.[26] Dery likewise argues that the urge to slough off the flesh, whether found in cyberpunk fiction or scientific speculations, is rooted in the mind-body dualism of Christianity: "The Christian worldview that underwrites Western culture overlays this physical disgust with a moral revulsion." He then cites D. H. Lawrence's comments that Christianity, and especially St. Paul, is the enemy of sensual life because of "his belief that the flesh is the cause of corruption."[27]

These criticisms sadly misunderstand the biblical view, which dignifies the physical universe. Genesis tells us that God created everything out of nothing by his word, and that it was "good."[28] For the Christian worldview, unlike Gnosticism, creation is not a bad idea. There is no fall into materiality. Humans are created out of the dust of the earth by the Spirit of God.[29] They are animated by the Spirit (not the earth), yet they are of the earth and are referred to as "wonderfully made."[30]

The entrance of sin and evil into the world was the result of humans rejecting God's rightful authority; it had nothing to do with being embodied or earth-bound. The results of the Fall of humanity affect every area of created life, but they do not render creation intrinsically evil or beyond the reach of God's redeeming grace. The Apostle Paul's negative references to "the flesh" do not refer to the body as such, as the Greek text makes clear, but to the sinful nature of all humans since the Fall. Sin is primarily a spiritual matter, not a physical condition.[31] Satan and demons (fallen angels) are not embodied, yet are fundamentally evil. Biblically, the material body is not the *source* of ethical corruption; the will is the source.

The incarnation of God in Christ further reveals that the material world is not something to be rejected. "The Word became flesh and made his dwelling among us," writes the Apostle John.[32] By assuming a human nature, God identified with our plight in flesh, blood, and bone. Paul, whom D. H. Lawrence accuses of attacking the body, taught that Jesus Christ was "born of a woman,"[33] that he became a human servant for our spiritual liberation,[34] and that "the fullness of the Deity lives in bodily form" in Christ.[35] Paul also said to Christians, "Once you were alienated from God and were enemies in your minds, because of your evil behavior. But now he has reconciled you by Christ's physical body through [his] death."[36] Jesus' sacrificial, atoning work was material as well as spiritual.

This, of course, the Gnostics could not accept—nor could they accept the biblical teaching that Jesus rose from the dead in a physical body in which he ate food, touched and spoke with people, and so forth. Christianity is not Gnosticism; it does not condemn materiality or the physical body as intrinsically evil or defective. Paul even warned of people who loathe the body and engage in pseudospiritual asceticism. These people wrongly forbid marriage and certain foods, "which God created to be received with thanksgiving by those who believe and know the truth. For everything that God created is good, and nothing is to be rejected if it is received with thanksgiving."[37]

The physical realm will be perfected in redeemed humanity's final state. Both the Hebrew Scriptures[38] and the New Testament disclose that, just as Christ rose from the dead in a perfected material body, so one day will Christians rise to eternal, embodied life freed from decay and the pollutions of sin. The immortality of the eternally disembodied soul is a Hellenistic notion, not a Hebraic one. The Bible does teach that the soul temporarily exists apart from the body during the time between one's physical death and the resurrection of the dead;[39] the final state, however, is embodied—both in heaven and in hell. Christians are free from the frantic quest to immortalize themselves through technological resurrections because their physical resurrection is as certain as that of Christ himself, who appeared after his death giving "many convincing proofs that he was alive."[40] His resurrection is the prototype of the resurrection of the believer in the age to come.[41]

In biblical teaching, matter is something not to be escaped but redeemed. The God of the Scriptures will be satisfied with nothing less than a radically reconstructed universe that perfectly reflects his unsurpassing greatness.[42] Christians, therefore, can appreciate the good gifts of creation without becoming materialists; they can believe in spiritual reality without degrading the physical dimension. In Christ, the Word has become flesh; we need not refuse earth in order to serve heaven. Clearly the teachings of biblical Christianity do not lie at the root of the modern, high-tech assault on the body.

HONORING THE PHYSICAL PRESENCE

In this age of disembodied communication in cyberspace, how should we honor and respect the physical presence of persons? Cyberspace, if used wisely, need not eclipse the materiality of persons in God's creation, but it must be treated with special care. We find the importance of the personal and the physical in the Apostle John's letters, written long before the discovery of electronic communication. In addressing "the chosen lady and her children," John warns of deceivers who deny that Jesus came in the flesh. He concludes by writing, "I have much to write to you, but I do not want to use paper and ink. Instead I hope to visit you and talk with you face to face, so that our joy may be complete."[43] John writes much the same to his "dear friend Gaius" when he says, "I have much to write you, but I do not want to do so with pen and ink. I hope to see you soon, and we will talk face to face."[44]

These closing comments are not incidental. There is a dimension of intimacy and accountability that comes with a face-to-face, person-to-person encounter that is not available otherwise. John relishes this human aspect in his recounting of his relationship with Jesus: "That which was from the beginning, which we have heard, which we have seen with our eyes, which we have looked at and our hands have touched—this we proclaim concerning the Word of life."[45] It is for good reason that James, Peter, and John extended "the right hand of fellowship" to Paul;[46] Paul and Peter urged Christ's people to "greet one another with a holy kiss";[47] and the New Testament repeatedly speaks of the practice of the "laying on of hands" for healing and commissioning ministries.[48]

Michael Heim rejects the Christian worldview, but his comments are on target:

> Today's computer communication cuts the physical face out of the communication process. Computers stick the windows of the soul behind monitors, headsets, and datasuits. . . . The living non-representable face is the primal source of responsibility, the direct, warm link between private bodies. Without directly meeting others physically, our ethics languishes. Face-to-face communication, the fleshly bond between people, supports a long-term warmth and loyalty, a sense of obligation for which the computer-mediated communities have not yet been tested.[49]

The lack of physical connectedness has been credited for explaining the phenomenon of "flaming" online. A "flame" is a vicious insult that is sent through e-mail, posted in a chat room or database, or contributed to a MOO or MUD. I myself learned this the hard way when I posted a message on a Christian bulletin board defending the egalitarian view of women and men in the church.[50] (I may have been asking for trouble, I suppose.) I was immediately assailed by someone who refused to reveal his offline identity, but who had no compunction about repeatedly attacking my spiritual and intellectual integrity—even after I asked him to stop sending messages. I can't imagine this mystery person carrying on this way in person or even over the phone.

Moreover, the rapidity and immediacy of e-mail seem to encourage an emotional discharge and superficiality that would be less likely even in letters, because they require more physical involvement at every stage of composition—printing out the letter on paper, signing it, folding it, stuffing it in an envelope, sealing the envelope, and carrying it to the mail box. This gives the writer more time and physical contact that allows him to reflect on matters that are (literally) "at hand" and "in hand" before committing the letter to the mail. The recipient of the letter is correspondingly involved at a physical dimension unknown in cyberspace. She handles the letter, breaks the seal, touches it as she reads, and then either saves it or throws it away. She might even send back a perfumed letter.

The physical and human aspects of traditional mail have other advantages. Traditional mail allows for some mistakes and near-misses because human souls read the addresses. But the computer mediation of cyberspace correspondence allows for no such ambiguity or fuzziness, because computers cannot discern meaning. The e-mail address must be letter-perfect to have any chance of arriving at its intended destination. It is all or nothing.

Furthermore, cybermail can backfire in ways undreamed of by the post office. One day I received several dozen e-mail messages, but none of them were for me. The next day it got worse. A ministry I had e-mailed was trying to use a program to send automatic e-mail messages to their mailing list. But the program had been set up wrongly and was sending every message originally sent to the ministry back to every person on the mailing list! I received not only messages intended for the ministry, but also messages complaining that people were getting messages that had been sent to the ministry. I even received my own complaining messages back again! After a few days of this highly recursive error, a very embarrassed message arrived from the ministry, saying that the program had been adjusted to cut off the e-mail avalanche. No single letter sent through "snail mail" could ever have such ramifications. Snails are slower, but safer.[51]

As we consider the benefits and drawbacks of e-mail, bulletin boards, and the rest, we should be like the young Solomon before the Lord and ask for wisdom first, foremost, and always.[52] Like Solomon we must refuse the lure of power, status, and wealth, and seek God's mind on how this alluring medium will shape us, our families, our churches, our nation, and our world. This will be the challenge addressed throughout the rest of this book.

3

THE BOOK, THE SCREEN, AND THE SOUL

OURS IS AN AGE INFATUATED WITH, addicted to, and voraciously hungry for ever-increasing doses of information. The promise of cyberspace, and particularly of the Internet, is that it will usher the much-vaunted information age into its own. More people can have greater access to more information more often. Data becomes transportable at hypervelocities—hence the term "snail mail" to refer to the postal service, as opposed to electronic-mail. The screen becomes the window of the soul, exposing a vista of previously unavailable or hard-to-find information. All we need to do is point, click, and take it in. In just a few key strokes we can link up with thousands of databases, Web pages, and other information cornucopias. Those who are not online are not in-the-know; they are sometimes called PONAs, people of no account.

IGNORANCE AND KNOWLEDGE

Ignorance is often an impediment in a fallen world. When a lack of knowledge is the primary obstacle in a particular case, the dissemination of pertinent information is a God-send. The earth has been a place of scarcity ever since it was cursed,[1] and knowledge is a resource subject to scarcity as much as resources such as food, water, gainful employment, intelligence, and housing. Ignorance may mean death, and knowledge may save lives.

Zhu Ling, a chemistry student at Peking University, mysteriously fell into a coma; one month later, her doctors still had not determined the cause of her illness. A friend of the young woman, one of the few students with access to the Internet, posted the following SOS message to a number of medical newsgroups on April 10, 1995:

> This is Peking University in China, a place of those dreams of freedom and democracy. However, a young, 21-year-old student has become very sick and is dying. The illness is very rare. Though they have tried, doctors at the best hospitals in Beijing cannot cure her; many do not even know what illness it is. So now we are asking the world—can somebody help us?[2]

A description of her symptoms was sent out over the Internet, and a diagnosis was quickly proposed by American physicians. It was thallium poisoning. The Chinese doctors were initially reluctant to take this information seriously, but eventually followed the advice received through e-mail and saw the young woman begin to recover from the poisoning. Without the Internet, the physicians in Peking probably would not have been able to arrive at an effective treatment plan. A special Web page has been set up for Zhu Ling, providing detailed medical information (including photos of her brain MRI and chest X-rays!) as well as personal updates on her condition which—as of fifteen months after her treatment began—is not fully improved. The medical potential for diagnosis and treatment through the use of computer technology is tremendous for physicians, researchers, and interested laypeople.[3]

As communications media develop, knowledge becomes more widely available and certain aspects of scarcity are diminished, often with profound results—whether medical, political, spiritual, or otherwise. Rulers of totalitarian regimes protect their power by making knowledge scarce and by limiting the opportunities for people to distribute information among themselves. In the former Soviet Union, photocopy machines and all other information technologies were strictly controlled by the government. Much of the USSR's undoing came with the liberalization of these policies. Once the word got out, an already beleaguered empire fell.

Computer technologies offer great potential for communicating with those who would not otherwise be quickly and easily accessible. For instance, I regularly write e-mail to friends in Brazil. We encourage each other in the faith, exchange prayer requests, and bring each other up to date on our ministries. Such books as *The Christian Cyberspace Companion* by Jason Baker are helpful guides to understanding and harnessing the sometimes esoteric workings of cyberspace for Christian endeavors.[4]

Moreover, the Internet makes important resources more easily available. In researching this book, I have downloaded dozens of articles and online interviews concerning cyberspace. I also write a column on apologetics, which is posted on the Internet. Through this, I have interacted with several people on important questions concerning the Christian faith. We have e-mailed each other, and I have sent out materials and lecture tapes through the postal service to encourage them. For these kinds of uses, I am thankful.

SENTIENCE, SENSIBILITIES, AND THE SOUL

But as Jacques Ellul has warned, the initial exuberance over a new technology often masks the problems that come to be known only later, oftentimes when it is too late to make important corrections. The positive effects are usually immediate, otherwise there would be no market for the technology. The deleterious effects appear more subtly over time, and tend to be ignored or denied in the mass marketing efforts. Moreover, these negative effects may not seem related to the new technology at first. Who originally thought that television would produce couch potatoes? Who knew that industrialization would alter family life forever?[5]

We should aim to be wise skeptics who realize that something is wrong with everything in a fallen world,[6] that things are rarely as good as they may seem initially, and that finite and fallen knowers can never accurately predict all the effects of a new mode of life. As Proverbs adjures us, "There is a way that seems right to a person, but its end is the way to death."[7] Second thoughts and second opinions are the way of wisdom: "The first to present his case seems right, till another comes forward and questions him."[8]

When information is conveyed through cyberspace, the medium shapes the message, the messenger, and the receiver. It shapes the entire culture. To understand this shaping function, we need to distinguish between the propositional content of a message and its conditions of sentience (its ambiance of awareness).[9] The propositional content concerns the factual assertions in any message or statement irrespective of its medium. For instance, the affirmation "Jesus is Lord" can be uttered out loud in a church service, written in a letter, found in Scripture, painted on a billboard, spoken live on the radio, sent in an e-mail message to a believer, or posted within an apologetic argument on an online bulletin board for Baha'is. In every situation, the statement objectively means the same thing. The conditions of sentience, however, differ in each case and affect how the message will be perceived. These conditions affect our very souls—as can be seen from a comparison of the book with the screen.

The nature of the book itself shapes our souls. Literary critic Sven Birkerts, who fears that the book is losing its cultural power, explains its peculiar virtues:

> The order of print is linear, and is bound to the logic of the imperatives of syntax. Syntax is the substance of discourse, a mapping of the ways that the mind makes sense through language. Print communication requires the active engagement of the reader's attention, for reading is fundamentally an act of translation. Symbols are turned into their verbal referents and these are in turn interpreted. . . . Print also posits a time axis; the turning of pages, not to mention the vertical descent down the page, is a forward-moving succession, with earlier contents at every point serving as a ground for what follows. Moreover the printed material is static—it is the reader, not the book, that moves forward. The physical arrangements of print are in accord with our traditional sense of history. Materials are layered; they lend themselves to rereading and to sustained attention. The pace of reading is variable, with progress determined by the reader's focus and comprehension.[10]

Birkerts correlates the nature of the book with the act of reading; together these constitute the conditions of sentience. In an essay called "The Book as a Container of Consciousness," novelist William H. Gass explains how the physicality of a book affects our reception of its message:

> That the size of type, the quality of paper, the weight of what the hands hold, the presence and placement of illustration, the volume's age, evidence of wear and tear, previous ownership and markings, sheer expense, have no affect upon the reader, and do not alter the experience of the text, is as absurd as supposing that . . . ice cream licks identically from cone or spoon or dish or dirty finger."[11]

These conditions of sentience in turn engender sensibilities—the perceptual and intellectual habits that we typically take for granted. Birkerts understands sensibility (which he puts in the singular) as "a refinement or cultivation of presence; it refers to the part of the inner life that is not given, but fashioned: a defining, if cloudy, complex of attitudes, predilections, and honed responses."[12] Our sensibilities encompass *how* we think as much as *what* we think; they draw our attention toward some things and away from others.

The stewardship of the senses is no small matter in our information-overcrowded world.[13] Our perceptual and intellectual capacities are limited; we cannot possibly handle the ever-increasing quantities of information. Therefore our sensibilities serve as our filters and our guides; they are the editors of the soul that direct our orientation toward good or evil. As Simone Weil said, "If we turn our mind toward the good, it is impossible that little by little the whole soul will not be attracted thereto in spite of itself."[14] The writer of Hebrews further elaborates on this when commending those who are mature in their thinking because their "faculties have been trained by practice to distinguish good from evil," unlike those who are still infants in their discernment.[15] Jesus also underscored the importance of developing appropriate sensibilities when he declared: "The eye is the lamp of the body. If your eyes are good, your whole body will be full of light. But if your eyes are bad, your whole body will be full of darkness."[16] Good eyes behold truth and enlighten the soul. Bad eyes, conversely, leave a person in the darkness.

INSCRIBED VERSUS EVANESCENT WORDS

Neil Postman argues that American culture has been molded by the book in an unprecedented way. The American veneration for literature in the eighteenth and nineteenth centuries produced what Postman calls the "typographic mind." This mind pursues logical coherence and intellectual depth; it is impatient with superficiality but willing to endure long and complex arguments for the sake of finding truth. Postman says:

> Almost all of the characteristics we associate with mature discourse were amplified by typography, which has the strongest possible bias toward exposition: a sophisticated ability to think conceptually, deductively and sequentially; a high valuation of reason and order; an abhorrence of contradiction; a large capacity for detachment and objectivity; and a tolerance for delayed response.[17]

Mature discourse is rare in our age of incivility and intellectual impatience. Much of the blame, as Postman and others have argued, can be placed upon television.

When a culture moves from typography to an image-based medium as its dominant and normative mode of expression, the very concepts of truth, reason, and evidence shift profoundly. Joshua Meyrowitz, a professor of communication at the University of New Hampshire, comments about his students: "They tend to have an image-based standard of truth. If I ask, 'What evidence supports your view or contradicts it?' they look at me as if I came from another planet." Why is this? "It's very foreign to them to think in terms of truth, logic, consistency and evidence."[18] Might this same erosion of the idea of truth and the ideals of logic, evidence, and consistency be perpetuated in cyberspace?

Receiving information through the computer is not identical to receiving information from books, although they both involve text. Many, however, are oblivious to the importance of this change in the conditions of sentience. For instance, newspaper columnist Charles Krauthammer has written that "while text will survive video, paper will not survive the computer. At the turn of the century text will forever leave paper and take up residence on-line." Krauthammer is not worried, though, since "clay tablets gave way to papyrus, sheepskin scrolls to bound books, illuminated manuscripts to Gutenberg type."[19]

Krauthammer's comments neglect the differences between inscription on objects (papyrus, sheepskin, bound book, illuminated manuscripts, Gutenberg type) and the insubstantiality of the screen. The screen contains words that appear and disappear at will (or sometimes against the will of the bewildered user). Any one screen may contain innumerable words because the words are not inscribed upon a surface; they appear on and are easily deleted from a monitor. The differences are highlighted by the bad joke about the stupid secretary who made corrections on a screen by using white-out. Words typed on a screen are not inscribed on an independent, imprintable object and thus require no white-out to remove or revise. They are evanescent, ephemeral—lacking in substantial rootedness or stability.

The inscription of words on surfaces, whether through handwriting or printing, gives them a kind of weight and identity. Novelist John Updike elicits just the right philosophical categories when he says that "there's something about the sensation of ink on paper that is in some sense a thing, a *phenomenon* rather than an *epiphenomenon*."[20] That is, the book's message is materially embedded as a phenomenon. The book is literally stained with meaning, nearly unerasable; it stands alone. The varying content of the screen, however, is an epiphenomenon because it depends on electricity and is completely erasable, just as a shadow has no independent existence apart from an object and light. The screen's content cannot stand alone. A power failure is enough to deface it or erase it entirely, and a software failure can lock up the material somewhere deep in the bowels of the silicon.

WORDS OF WEIGHT

When Yahweh made his moral will known to the people he brought out of Egypt, he inscribed the Ten Commandments on two stone tablets, which were delivered in person by Moses to the people. They "were inscribed on both sides, front and back. The tablets were the work of God; the writing was the writing of God, engraved on the tablets."[21] With this divine action, the Creator forever dignified the written word. Even after Moses broke the tablets in response to the Israelites' worship of the golden calf, God directed him to make two more tablets, so that the law of the covenant could be written down again.[22] It was not sufficient for Moses simply to repeat what he had heard God pronounce; rather the words were recorded literally in stone to signify their perpetuity and incorruptibility. Likewise, in the Book of Revelation, after John beheld the transfigured and ascended Christ, he was instructed to "Write, therefore, what you have seen, what is now and what will take place later."[23]

Christians and Jews are "people of the book" because they believe God revealed his truth to the varied writers of Scripture in words that ought to be conserved, understood, and obeyed. Throughout history, the books of the Bible have been meticulously copied, recopied, and preserved so that the faithful would have the Holy Scriptures at their disposal. Significantly, when emissaries of the gospel message enter an exclusively oral culture, they carefully devise a written language so that the Bible can be inscribed and treasured by these people in their own language. And when the Bible has not been translated into a culture's written language, missionaries immediately set about the task of providing these people with the written word of God. Clearly, the physical inscription of truth is central to God's revelation to humanity.

The raw physicality of the written word is literally felt in all books. Literary critic Erik Ness comments, "Many readers love the very physical essence of books—the weft of ideas, the warp of words, the loom of paper all bound in leather. No computer screen can match this visceral pleasure. Screen glare, a clattering keyboard and a humming hard drive are no equal for the magical heft of a book."[24] By comparison, the effect of words on a screen—whether written or read—can depreciate the depth and gravity of language itself. Since I do not turn any pages but instead scroll through material, I may lose the sense of linearity reinforced by the book and other printed matter.

Moreover, the screen has less involvement with physical history than does the book. I can easily move about a text electronically without fingering pages. I can "call up" a screen that displays my previous work or material I have downloaded. Yet the screen text does not bear the marks of the physical world and the human touch. No pages are worn, no highlighting appears, no distinctive smells are evident. The screen is clean, always the same; it has no history and little personality. It may be a receptacle for text and images, but it is imprinted by none of them. Without power, it is a mere blank, a dead conduit—and rather ugly at that.

Writing on the screen, as opposed to composing on paper, may also encourage a certain carelessness by virtue of its ease of execution. Birkerts observes that, when writing consisted of putting words to paper,

> The path between [the writer's] impulse and inscription was made thornier by the knowledge that errors meant having to retrace steps and do more work. The writer was more likely to test the phrasing on the ear, to edit mentally before committing to the paper. The underlying momentum was toward the right, irrevocable expression.[25]

By comparison, word processing allows for immediate expression, the freedom from linearity (I can work at any point in the document), and revision with little pain. Heim comments that "the power at your finger tips tempts you to believe that faster is better, that ease means instant quality."[26]

Although some believe that the ease of writing and the mobility of data might yield a literary revival, a pioneering veteran of the Internet who has logged countless hours online, Clifford Stoll, disagrees.

> Instead of an Internet-inspired renaissance, mediocre writing and poorly thought-out arguments roll into my modem. E-mail and postings to network newsgroups are frequently ungrammatical, misspelled, and poorly organized. After trolling up and down the Usenet, from alt.best-of-usenet to zer.z-netz.telecom.modem, I rarely find prose that's articulate and creative.[27]

My own less extensive experience online chimes in with Stoll's views; he calls the notion that cyberspace will produce a literary revival "one of the more pernicious myths of the online world."[28]

LIBRARIES WITHOUT WALLS

A sense of history links souls together, providing purpose, stability, and identity. Many in cyberspace, however, appear to be rootless individuals divorced from the events of the past. Theodore Rozsak nails down their mentality well:

> I sometimes suspect that computer enthusiasts, committed to a dynamic technology that seems always to be moving forward toward ever more spectacular breakthroughs, exist in a sort of posthistoric limbo. Perhaps this is the most appealing feature of cyberspace: it has no past, only a future. It imposes no responsibilities or obligations, only bright promises and happy diversions.[29]

In light of this, it is no surprise that Bill Gates's best-selling promotion of the expected information superhighway is called *The Road Ahead*. For Gates and many others, history began with the advent of the personal computer, and the best (especially for Microsoft) is yet to come.

Cyberspace poses yet another hazard to historical memory—the decay and obsolescence of digital documents. The synthesis of silicon and electricity has many mind-boggling benefits but also dangerous detriments. Ironically, although computers are praised as the great receptacles and dispensers of information, they are far less durable and trustworthy than what you now have in your hands and before your eyes. But before making this case, we need to look at the digitopian vision.

Albert Gore, a leading cheerleader for the information super-highway, dreams of a day when school children, along with every-one else, will be able to plug into the entire Library of Congress at any time, surf the newly digitized collection, and download what-ever is wanted.[30] Some even speak of the end of the traditional library, because anything that might be needed will be available online. If I want a book that is checked out of a library, I have to wait for it because an object cannot be in two places at once. It is different with data. We can all download a document simultane-ously—at least, if we have the proper hardware, software, and know-how. No books need be in sight. Documents can also be customized through hypertext functions (as discussed in the next chapter).

Some thirty years ago, Ted Nelson, computer entrepreneur and inventor of hypertext technology, conceived of a project that would render books obsolete. Xanadu was envisioned as a "vast database of the corpus of English literature"[31] that would be made available to consumers as a "fast information outlet, doing for data what McDon-alds did for burgers."[32] Xanadu may never fulfill its promises, given both copyright problems and the expensive and time-consuming nature of the project. Wired described it as "the longest running vaporware project in the history of computing—a thirty-year saga of rabid prototyping and heart-slashing despair."[33] Cyberhype often breaks on the rocks of real life, but many still yearn for the digitization of documents for greater accessibility and malleability.

The book, much-maligned in some cyberspace circles, has a great advantage over all the visions of libraries without walls and knowl-edge without pages. Unelectric and low-tech, the book requires min-imal physical retrieval skills—find a comfortable chair, open the book, turn the pages, and read. Moreover, a book can last for hun-dreds of years. An acquaintance of mine purchased an eighteenth-century volume by philosopher David Hume. The binding was still intact, the print legible, and the script readable. An article in Sci-entific American on the problem of preserving digital documents fea-tured a picture of the first printed copy (1609) of "Sonnet 18" by Shakespeare, which is well preserved and readable.[34] The final couplet relates to the preservation of documents:

So long as men can breathe or eyes can see,
So long lives this, and this gives life to thee.[35]

Digital documents may not fair so well, precisely because they are technologically "advanced." The article warns that these "documents are far more fragile than paper, placing the chronicle of our entire period in jeopardy."[36] How much will be flushed down the digital memory hole?

The data stored in computers must be translated into human languages to be understood. Prying it out of the machines, especially as they age, may be no simple matter. Although the basic structure of the book—pages, binding, cover—has not changed for centuries, the programs and machines for storing and retrieving digital data change at a blinding rate. For example, my wife and I each wrote two books on a KayPro computer I bought in 1983. KayPro is now long out of business, in part because its operating system, CP/M, failed to become an industry standard. The disks on which our books are digitally stored are now essentially worthless because newer computers cannot read material from a CP/M system. Translation programs are available, but the process is imperfect and time consuming. But because the material that we wrote on our old KayPro has been translated into the written word and printed in book form, it is both accessible and durable. Even after the books go out of print, their physical existence will continue because of libraries, used book stores, and photocopiers.

One may argue that since computer operating systems and other programs are now standardized and technologies are improving, problems of data retrieval will lessen. This is not necessarily true for several reasons. First, what is standardized today may be unreadable tomorrow. Stoll points out that although a CD-ROM has a long life span, it may not be readable in a short time because the technologies change so rapidly.[37] Try playing a 78-rpm record or an 8-track tape today. The recordings may be in mint condition, but they are about as valuable as gold locked in a safe that no one can crack, because the devices needed to unlock their treasures are scarce and no longer produced.

Second, even if machines exist to read digital materials, the materials themselves may decay quickly when compared with the longevity of printed documents. Computer scientist Jeff Rothenberg notes that "the contents of most digital media evaporate long before words written on high-quality paper."[38] Although he gives some technical advice on how to preserve the bits from decay and to ensure

their retrievability with newer technologies, he is not entirely san-
guine about the prospects.

Several near misses have already terrified data managers. The
1960 U.S. Census data was almost entirely lost when the tapes on
which it was stored became obsolete far faster than anticipated. Tapes
from the Department of Health and Human Services, and files of the
National Commission on Marijuana and Drug Abuse and other agencies, were also in jeopardy.[39] NASA has twenty thousand seven-track
tapes containing data on space exploration that can only be read on
the outdated seven-track tape drive. When their drive broke in 1992,
NASA only found one other drive in existence.[40]

The time, technical skill, and expense involved in updating the
means of proper data storage is considerable. Don Norman of Apple
Computer suggests that we may need an entirely new field of study,
"cyber-archaeology."[41] Drugs and many processed foods come with
expiration dates clearly written on their packaging, but digital storage
is a trickier proposition by far. Ted Nelson, a computer pioneer himself, admits that "the so-called information age is really the age of
information lost."[42]

Novelist William Gibson may have sensed this ephemerality
when he wrote an autobiographical story called "Agrippa" on computer disk in 1992. Only thirty-five copies were released, all of which
were programmed to erase the story as it was played. A pirated edition
made it onto the Internet, however.[43] Another case of "information
lost" concerns what is possibly the first hypertext novel: Rob Swigart's
Portal, published in 1986. Designed specifically for the computers of
its day, the work became mostly unreadable when new models quickly
superseded the old.[44] The digitized word does not abide forever.[45]

No doubt digitopians will maintain that digital immortality is only
a few discoveries away; postdated checks, however, are just too risky
when it is a matter of preserving a record of our history. If everything
goes digital, then everything will be exposed to new and unpredictable
dangers. Furthermore, as we argued earlier, the word on the screen carries with it different sensibilities than the word on the page. Stoll dis-
putes the "concealed proposition" of those anxious to digitize everything,
"that you can take information, change the format, and still have the
same thing. That's true for data. Not true for information."[46]

The ultimate archival institution is the library building: furnished with books and other printed matter as well as chairs and tables, full of people looking at books, talking to one another, and joining the communal memory. Books, despite their inert status and lack of electronic charisma, are living things that join us to a larger community of souls, as John Milton knew well.

> For books are not absolutely dead things, but do contain a potency of life in them to be as active as that soul was whose progeny they are; nay, they do preserve as in a vial the purest efficacy and extraction of that living intellect that bred them.[47]

Libraries without walls, even if possible, would be libraries without books, which would be akin to food without taste and without much nutrition. Walls bring people together for specific purposes; they bracket areas of concern and provide room (literally) for important patterns of human association. A friendly chat at the card catalog (assuming your library still has one[48]), the magazine racks, or the book stacks may result in a treasure of new knowledge—or perhaps even a lifelong friendship.

Because cyberspace has no walls it gives the illusion of almost infinite possibility. Finite beings, nonetheless, need finite and findable possibilities; we need walls as well as doors. The soul is impoverished when it is severed from a sense of history and cultural continuity, no matter how stuffed with information it may be. Cyberspace, for all its innovations, speed, and power, may be less durable and hospitable than many surmise. Even as it increases data connections, cyberspace could seduce and ultimately betray our souls.

4

HYPERTEXT REALITIES AND EFFECTS

THE CHARACTER OF THE COMPUTER SCREEN, the strange powers of word processing, and the almost ubiquitous Internet tend to reinforce certain postmodernist themes that may undermine Christian sensibilities and a biblical worldview. One much-heralded technology, known as hypertext, is especially potent in its ability to fragment literary meaning and textual authority. Hypertext allows users to have access to various parts of a document, or of several documents at once, by merely pointing and clicking. This function tends to encourage a swift skimming, surfing, or scanning of information according to nonlinear associations. The prefix *hyper* refers to an added dimension: there is an extra element to the texts in that they can be navigated, manipulated, and even distorted by this new technology.[1]

UNDOING THE TEXT

Instant access to all kinds of information may corrode a sense of coherence and meaning if the information is not put into an appropriate framework. This can be illustrated from television, still the dominant medium today. Neil Postman points out that although "the whole point of language is to provide a world of intellectual and emotional continuity and predictability," many of his students do not understand the most basic principles of logical thought. Postman believes their intellectual incoherence derives from television, "which tells you that there was a rape in New York and then it tells you there was an earthquake in Chile and then it tells you that the Mets beat the Cardinals."[2] The sensibilities engendered by language as expressed in book form are overthrown when the book is replaced by a medium that discourages the meaningful arrangement of information into a coherent narrative or argument.

The recent popularity of interactive CD-ROMs signals the attempt to combine text with image in educational and/or entertaining ways.[3] With these technologies, one can point and click one's way around numerous images, texts, and video and audio clips on subjects as varied as classical music, Marshall McLuhan, and Monty Python's Flying Circus (a British comedy group).

But as Jacques Ellul has noted, in most modern communication the image tends to "humiliate the word" because the language text is overshadowed and controlled by the nonlinguistic elements such as photographs, animation, cartoons, drawings, and all manner of graphics.[4] The "multimedia" environment supposedly enhances learning by multiplying the types of sensory inputs. In the process, however, the nature of the text tends to change. Rather than standing alone as the center of whatever meaning is conveyed, the text is cropped, simplified, and assimilated into the graphical environment.

As CD-ROMs use hypertext technologies, there may be little or no linear flow to whatever texts are selected. One can jump around wherever one wants. The CD-ROM becomes what Paul Roberts calls "an egoless supertext" of assorted textual patches, sound bites, and images.[5] The idea of one author is absorbed by the technological functions. Roberts writes of his initiation into the lucrative but distressing world of writing for CD-ROMs. Once an aspiring environmental ethics writer, he laments over the superficiality of what he, "the blurbmeister," is assigned to write, such as a hundred words on Mozart. Digitally glorified blurbs replace discourse. The immediacy of sensory stimulation replaces the time and effort required to wrest meaning from an inert text.

Discourse is the intellectual process whereby we attend to linguistic meaning, pursue possible interpretations, compare arguments, and come to conclusions of various intellectual strengths. The tendency of the CD-ROM is to undermine discourse and replace it with a kind of information distraction. As we surf from node to node, we get the impression that we have learned something. But because most CD-ROMs are so visually oriented, they do not teach the discipline of reasoned discourse.

Ellul observes that unlike spoken or written discourse, "visual representation is the easy, efficient, quick path. It allows us to grasp a totality in a single glance, without any need to break up a thing and to analyze it." Analysis is paralyzed by the domination of randomly selected images. "It is much easier to let oneself be captivated or impressed by an image than to follow an oral [or written] demonstration."[6] Granted these realities, interactive CD-ROMs will lean toward the entertaining and away from the educational. While encouraging digital tourism, they tend to discourage the development of skills in careful reading and writing.

Reva Basch, an Internet researcher who calls herself a "cybrarian," confesses that her extensive scanning of screens online shapes a sensibility that spills over into her book reading. When reading for pleasure, she says "I just can't keep my eyes still. I have to remind myself to slow down and say 'Hey, you're reading for style, not content, stop browsing, start reading.' "[7] The soul in cyberspace may easily habituate itself to browsing, data-surfing, and skimming in exchange for analysis, reflection, and discourse.

A DOUBLE-EDGED TECHNOLOGY

Many readers may be complaining at this point, "But what of the tremendous accessibility of information that hypertext and CD-ROMs provide? It helps overcome the scarcity of knowledge you mentioned earlier." Indeed it does. As I was reading Stephen Carter's provocative book *Integrity*, I ran across a citation from Augustine's *City of God*, which I wanted to use in this book: "The peace of the rational soul is the ordered agreement of knowledge and action."[8] Unfortunately, Carter's footnote failed to list the exact reference from the *City of God*, and I did not know where to find it. Since I hesitate to give references to a secondary work in this way (although I just did in the endnote), I immediately wished for a hypertext index to the *City of God* that would allow me to type in a few words and come up with the exact location. I do not know of such a source, but should there be one, I would be the first to use it. Let me give another favorable example.

Theologian Thomas Oden exults that through a CD-ROM reader he can "search all the texts of ancient Greek literature for a particular word in minutes, a task that would have taken years if done by hand."[9] There is no reason to fret about Thomas Oden losing a sense of coherence and meaning in life because of the vast ocean of information available at his keyboard. He is a Christian intellectual whose sensibilities and worldview have been matured in the study, in the library, and in the classroom through decades spent with thousands of books. His use of retrieval technologies simply augments his desire for greater understanding.

But a typographic orientation is not inscribed in the souls of most Americans today, especially younger people. Consider an example of an unforeseen effect of our intensely image-oriented culture on mathematics students. Many educators hail computer graphics as key in mathematics education. But a *Scientific American* article, "The Death of Proof," reported that in a meeting of mathematicians and high school teachers, the teachers disagreed with the mathematicians' claim that "proofs are crucial to ensure that a result is true." They

> pointed out that students no longer considered traditional, axiomatic proofs to be as convincing as, say, visual arguments. "The high school teachers overwhelmingly declared that most students now (Nintendo/joy-stick/MTV generation) do not relate to or see the importance of 'proofs' " the minutes of the meeting stated. Note the quotation marks around the word "proofs."[10]

Abstract logic seems to be losing its grip on a generation of visually oriented young people. This trend will likely be furthered by the kind of hypertext and CD-ROM technologies we have discussed. If so, our sensibilities will continue to be technologically manipulated to avoid logical reasoning and the idea of absolute truth.

For all its possible benefits when used wisely, the hypertext function is double-edged. One edge cuts out ignorance and opens up new vistas of knowledge; the other edge tends to eliminate the notion of a fixed text and a single author, and also lowers our level of attentiveness.

EXIT AUTHOR, ENTER AUTHORS

Because texts in cyberspace are so malleable and movable, we can easily lose the sense of a unitary author as the source of meaning. This shift in emphasis dovetails with the postmodernist or deconstructionist attack on objective meaning, on the legitimacy of comprehensive worldviews, and on the integrity of literary texts as expressing the determined intention of their authors. Philosopher Richard A. Lanham comments that "the open-ended screen text subverts traditional fantasies of a master narrative, or definitive reading, by presenting the reader with possibilities for changing fonts, zooming in and out, and rearranging and replacing text."[11] Lanham believes that the result is "a body of work active not passive, a canon not frozen in perfection but volatile with contending human motives."[12]

Journalist Benjamin Woolley observes that this viewpoint subverts the classical view, enshrined in the Bible, that books "are written to be read in the order and fashion set out by the author." Therefore, "books are not . . . the result of collaboration or negotiation; they are given by their authors so that they may be taken by their readers." This ancient arrangement "is part of a normally non-negotiable pact" between the author and reader, "which involves producing on the one part and consuming on the other."[13]

Similarly, novelist John Barth describes the "traditional job description of Author and Reader" as: "You don't like the restaurant? Then dine elsewhere—but stay out of my kitchen while I'm cooking for you, please, and I'll return the favor."[14] In other words, one may take issue with an author for any number of reasons, but one does so as a dissenting reader, not as a surrogate or surreptitious coauthor. A text is not a wax nose one may twist into any configuration. As Pascal said with regard to Scripture, "Anyone who wishes to give the meaning of Scripture without taking it from Scripture is the enemy of Scripture."[15]

The more "interactive" the computer technology, the more indeterminate and fuzzy the meaning of texts tends to become. What used to be called the "cut and paste" method (to hark back to a more physical endeavor) now becomes almost effortless and entirely frictionless. A pastiche of relative and subjective meanings replaces the unitary fabric of discoverable truth. Texts forfeit their weight and bearing, become uprooted, and float adrift in the arbitrary atmospheres of cyberspace.

The outcome of this fragmentation of the text is the elimination of the author and the inflation of the reader. Because postmodernists decry the tyranny of the author over the reader, they rejoice in these technologies. Robert Coover's comments are illustrative:

> With its webs of linked lexias [multiple paths between portions of texts], its networks of alternate routes (as opposed to print's fixed unidirectional page-turning), hypertext presents a radically divergent technology, interactive and polyvocal, favoring a plurality of

discourses over definitive utterance and freeing the reader from domination by the author. Hypertext reader and writer are said to become
co-learners or co-writers, as it were, fellow travelers in the mapping
and remapping of textual (and visual, kinetic, and aural) components, not all of which are provided by what used to be the author.[16]

Coover claims that this technology "*favors* a plurality of discourses," but of course does not demand it. As McLuhan famously
observed, however, "We become what we behold."[17] If our sensibilities
are set by the capacities of hypertext, we may begin to relinquish our
grip on the very notion of author-ity. Writing long before cyberspace
or modern deconstructionism emerged, C. S. Lewis warned of errant
literary critics who think that "everything [in literature] can be a symbol, or an irony, or an ambiguity." In so doing, they "easily find what
they want." We can become "so busy doing things with the work that
we give it too little chance to work on us. Thus increasingly we meet
only ourselves [in the text]."[18] To meet only ourselves in the text is
to shrink our world to the size of our selves and to imprison meanings in "the dungeon house of the ego," as Malcolm Muggeridge put
it.[19] For all Coover's talk of "the mapping and remapping of textual
components," such maps can only reflect the self; there is no territory beyond. This is akin to looking into a vanity mirror when lost
on the freeway. Narcissus has taken up digital residence in cyberspace.

Coover's description allows for and encourages the severing of the
author's intellectual intention from the body of his or her work. The
text is then dissected, disfigured, and expanded by other desiccated
texts, resulting in an ever-evolving corpus of technological anarchy
in which the author-reader dichotomy is shattered. As Woolley puts it,
"In cyberspace, everyone is an author, which means that no one is an
author: the distinction upon which it rests, the author distinct from
the reader, disappears. Exit author. . . ."[20] The idea of plot or argument
also disappears, notes computer scientist David Gelernter. Authors
labor earnestly to "make the narrative read a certain way, prove a particular point." Therefore, to "turn a book or a document into hypertext
is to invite readers to ignore exactly what counts—the story."[21]

The loss of the determinate author was exemplified by a cover
story on Marshall McLuhan in the January 1996 issue of *Wired* magazine. McLuhan (1911–80), listed in its masthead as the patron saint
of the magazine, was said to have consented to a channeled inter-

view—through the Internet, of course. A year previous to the article, someone identified only as Marshall McLuhan had begun posting messages on a popular mailing list called Zone. Gary Wolf conducted the interview over e-mail with this person called "Marshall." Wolf concluded that if this was not McLuhan, "it was a bot programmed with an eerie command of McLuhan's life and inimitable perspective."[22] (A "bot" is a program that simulates human interaction in cyberspace. We will take this up in chapter nine.) The "interview" was, in one sense, tongue-in-cheek because we know McLuhan is dead, and there was no New Age pretense of channeling him in a spiritistic sense. The responses of "Marshall," however, seem to be somewhat "in character" as a kind of intellectual impersonation of what the media guru might make of the cyberspace revolution.

The significance of this "interview" is the extent to which an actual author is removed or opaque. The impersonator is never identified; he or she comes from somewhere in cyberspace and impersonates McLuhan, who is not really the author of the responses. The introduction to the *Wired* article also tells us that McLuhan's later books themselves may have been more collaborations than works actually authored by him. Instead of a text rooted in an identifiable life, there remains only a free-floating text literally without author-ity. Like some kind of postmodern Cheshire cat, all that remains is a smirk or a wink, but no face.

THE LOSS OF THE ARTIST

The loss of the author is closely related to another cyberspace development, the loss of the artist. Musician and composer Brian Eno surmises that computer technologies will increasingly dethrone the inviolate artist and enthrone the listener as the ersatz composer who will arrange musical samples in various ways to suit his or her tastes. He believes that "the hypertext consciousness is spreading to things we take in, not only things we read."[23] In other words, everything is subject to subjective rearrangement, irrespective of any fixed meaning. Nicholas Negroponte sees the predicted "digital superhighway" as making "finished and unalterable art into a thing of the past. . . , which is not necessarily bad."[24] To some degree, this is already afoot. CD-ROMs such as Peter Gabriel's *Xplora* and Todd Rungren's *No World Order* "invite viewers/listeners to reassemble images and change tempo and mood, customizing tracks to their own tastes."[25] Gabriel believes the CD-ROM "will destroy the elite divide between those who can create and those who can't."[26]

This state of affairs suits Eno just fine; he rejects the classical view that "art objects are containers of some kind of aesthetic value," opting instead for the postmodernist perspective that "cultural objects have no notable identity outside of that which we confer upon them."[27] This, of course, is nihilism (albeit a cyberspace variation): nothing has any intrinsic value or meaning, everything can be rearranged, created, or destroyed without obligation to any normative design, pattern, or purpose. Friedrich Nietzsche, one who dared look deep into the abyss, declared that apart from our own subjective projections of value, "the nut of existence would be hollow."[28] All value is arbitrarily constructed by people who have no possible means of reaching aesthetic or ethical judgments that transcend their own sensory awareness.[29] Nazi art, anyone? Or how about Mona Lisa diapers?

DECONSTRUCTING THE DECONSTRUCTIONISTS

A simple test of the deconstructionist's "freeing of the text from its author" is the application of their own method to their own writings. Using hypertext, I will cut and paste the Coover quotation below and become his uninvited "co-writer" through a few deft omissions (indicated by ellipses).

> With its . . . unidirectional page-turning, hypertext presents a . . . technology of discourses . . . of definitive utterance. . . . Hypertext reader and writer are said to become . . . fellow travelers in the mapping and remapping of . . . components, . . . all of which are provided by . . . the author.

My unsolicited coauthorship confuses and contradicts the meaning of the authentic text, as Coover would immediately object. I could employ the same strategy on quotations from Brian Eno or Nicholas Negroponte, which would produce the same kind of outraged response. Had I injected my own textual additions into Coover's text, the distortions of meaning would have become even more nefarious, outrageous, and indefensible.

Certainly, the electronic availability of texts can augment knowledge when used responsibly, as when I took portions of some of my previously written articles and letters and inserted them in some chapters of this book. The transportability of the text was quite delightful in these cases, since the intrinsic meaning of the material was never in jeopardy. But when meaning itself is assailed, the situation becomes illogical and poisonous because the very concept of textual integrity and authorial intent collapses. There is no unified text and no one author.

Electronic fiction (or e-fiction) by its very definition lacks a singular author or text. Through hypertext, electronic "texts" are created and remain open to constant revision and elaboration by a host of author-readers, forming a literary world that lacks closure, structure, and coherence. Coover confesses the vertigo of it all:

> How do you move around in infinity without getting lost? The structuring of the [hypertext] space can be so compelling and confusing as to utterly absorb and neutralize the narrator and to exhaust the reader. And there is the related problem of filtering. With an unstable text that can be intruded upon by other author-readers, how do you, caught in the maze, avoid the trivial? How do you duck the garbage? Venerable novelistic values like unity, integrity, coherence, vision, voice, seem to be in danger.[30]

Indeed, how do you navigate "infinity" with integrity—unless you are infinite yourself, or possess a map from the Infinite? The unrooted myriad of words and ideas is aptly described as a "maze," something that is confining and perplexing because of its incoherence and indeterminacy. It is no wonder that cyberpunk writer William Gibson has dubbed cyberspace "an infinite cage."[31] This pseudoinfinity (virtual infinity) imprisons its participants, not through a constricting narrowness, but through an exhausting wideness.

COGNITIVE TOURISM

Another dangerous aspect of hypertext is its tendency to lower our level of attention through its ease of access. Cyberspace offers the promise of a kind of cognitive ubiquity—the world at our keyboard and screen—at the cost of depth. This encourages one to become a cognitive tourist, who visits many sites on the Net, downloads and combines many bits of data, but understands very little. Just as the tourist in physical space "gets there without the experience of having gone,"[32] the cognitive tourist of cyberspace may easily visit (and possibly record) information without digesting it. The one sees the land-scape with little understanding or participation; the other sees the datascape with equal oblivion, having transcended place and distance entirely. The modern tourist makes "stops" with little sense of actu-ally traveling between geographical points—given the comfort and speed of air travel and the slick, efficient packaging of vacation tours—while the cognitive tourist makes "data stops" with a mouse as his guide and a screen as the portal for the rush of incoming data.

French philosopher Paul Virilio aptly observes that we no longer even need to depart, because "*everything arrives* without our having to leave. But what 'arrives' is already no longer a stopover or the end of the trip; it is merely information, *information-world*, no, *information-universe!*"[33] The arrival of the information universe may not produce an understanding of reality. The Apostle Paul knew of this problem two thousand years ago when he spoke of those who are "always learning but never able to acknowledge the truth."[34]

The advice of the Stoic philosopher Seneca (4 B.C.–65 A.D.) on the art of reading and thinking hits home today. He warns that one's reading should dwell on the works of writers "whose genius is unques-tionable" instead of flitting from one book to the next, as is the case with people "who spend their whole life traveling abroad [and] end up having plenty of places where they can find hospitality but [have] no real friendships."[35] In another colorful analogy, Seneca responds to the idea that one should sample different books at different times: "Tasting one dish after another is the sign of a fussy stomach, and where the foods are dissimilar and diverse in range they lead to cont-amination of the system, not nutrition." He wisely sums it up: "To be everywhere is to be nowhere."[36] To adapt this to cyberspace, we might say, "To be virtually everywhere is to be literally nowhere."

More and more souls are being siphoned into the beckoning abyss of nowhere. As we have seen, the computer screen—despite its myriad enchantments—may not be a hot house for the soul. The book, that stubbornly unelectric artifact of pure typography, possesses resources conducive to the flourishing of the soul. A thoughtful read-ing of the printed text orients one to a world of order, meaning, and the possibility of knowing truth.

5

※※

THE FATE OF TRUTH IN CYBERSPACE

IN THE FIRST CHAPTERS we explored the ways in which cyberspace can sap the soul. Technologies, despite their diverse applications, are not neutral tools. They affect our lives in countless and often invisible ways. To become aware of our plight and find hope for our troubled souls, we must consider seriously the meaning of the machine. In the decentered self of assumed, online identities, the artificial is offered as the only option for the postmodern soul. There is no "real me," no trustworthy pattern for moral and spiritual improvement. All is negotiable, exchangeable, and multiple. Integrity becomes impossible; the ideal of virtuous character recedes even as the heart yearns for a self to call its own.

The disembodied context of cyberspace may also spark false hopes for a digital resurrection without the flesh, an escape into the datasphere. The abandonment of the book for the screen affects us profoundly as we lose the sense of coherence, linear order, authorship, and stable meaning that is engendered by the medium of the book and the act of reading. Given the sensibilities encouraged by the world of cyberspace, the quest for truth as the tonic for the soul becomes problematic.

The double edge of cyberspace technologies cuts even deeper than what we have seen thus far. What is the fate of truth in cyberspace? Will the torrential flow of information overcome crippling ignorance? Will online communication become the next great medium for evangelization? Will our increasing connectedness facilitate the sharing of truth to an unprecedented degree in history? What chances does truth have in cyberspace?

PURSUING TRUTH IN A WORLD OF ERROR

Centuries ago Pascal wrote that "Truth today is so obscure and error so established, that unless we love the truth, we will never know it."[1] Well before our technological age, Pascal pondered at length the plight of human knowledge in a world rife with error, deception, confusion, and stupidity. A key element in his argument for the Christian worldview is his insistence that skeptics, agnostics, and all unbelievers need to seek the truth earnestly—to love it above all other affairs, even if they have yet to lay hold of it. Pascal defines his project this way:

> I should . . . like to arouse in man the desire to find truth, to be ready, free from passion, to follow it wherever he may find it, real-izing how far his knowledge is clouded by passions. I should like him to hate concupiscence which automatically makes his deci-sions for him, so that it should not blind him when he makes his choice, nor hinder him once he has chosen.[2]

Pascal was well aware of the chains that keep us bound in untruths and the legion of excuses we have for dispensing with the search as too burdensome. "Those who do not love truth excuse themselves on the grounds that it is disputed and that very many people deny it. Thus their error is solely due to the fact that they love neither the truth nor charity, and so they have no excuse."[3] A desire for truth, whatever the personal cost, is key in stewarding one's senses and adjusting one's sensibilities for the reception of reality.

Another strategy for avoiding the truth is articulated by C. S. Lewis through the demon Screwtape, who advises a junior demon on the wiles of deception.

> Your man has been accustomed, ever since he was a boy, to having a dozen incompatible philosophies dancing about together inside his head. He doesn't think of doctrines as primarily "true" or "false," but as "academic" or "practical," "outworn" or "contemporary," "conventional or "ruthless." Jargon, not argument, is your best ally in keeping him from the Church.[4]

Screwtape further counsels Wormwood to keep his man from "the fatal habit of attending to universal issues and withdrawing his atten-tion from the stream of immediate sense experiences. Your business is to fix his attention on the stream."[5] The stream of immediate sensations, whether from "surfing the Net" or some other activity, usually does not lend itself to a consideration of the "universal issues" of the soul's origin, nature, duty, purpose, and destiny.

Pascal, the leading intellect of his day, wrote his warnings before the advent of any of the information technologies into which our lives are so tightly woven. He did, however, devise the first adding machine, which he constructed to help his father calculate taxes. The rudiments of this invention formed the beginnings of the computer, a device that not only extends our capacities for knowledge but encourages the avoidance of truth entirely. We should heed the words of Simone Weil who, in an essay called "The Needs of the Soul," wrote that "the need of truth is more sacred than any other need. Yet it is never mentioned."[6] If truth is the soul's deepest need and its greatest asset, it must resist the siren songs of cyberspace that would render the knowledge of truth impossible.[7]

THE TRUTH ABOUT TRUTH

When Pontius Pilate interrogated Jesus before his crucifixion, Jesus proclaimed, "Everyone on the side of truth listens to me."[8] To this, Pilate replied, "What is truth?" and immediately left Jesus' presence to address the Jews who wanted Christ crucified. As Francis Bacon wrote in his essay "On Truth": " 'What is truth?' said jesting Pilate; and would not stay for an answer."[9] Although we have no record of any reply from Jesus, Christians affirm that Pilate was staring Truth in the face, for Jesus had said earlier to his disciple Thomas, "I am the way, and the truth, and the life."[10]

This exchange raises the perennial question of the nature of truth. What does it mean for a statement to be true? Many post-modernist circles debate this subject as they question established views about truth being objective and knowable. And many outside academic discussions may be as cynical about truth as Pilate. "What is truth?" they smirk, without waiting for an answer. But unless we are clear about the notion of truth, any claim to truth—Christian or otherwise—will perplex more than enlighten.

The correspondence view of truth, held by the vast majority of philosophers and theologians throughout history until recently, is that any statement is true if and only if it corresponds to or agrees with factual reality. The statement, "The desk in my study is brown," is true only if there is a brown desk in my study. In this case the statement, "The desk in my study is not brown," is false. And its falsehood is not determined by subjective preference or majority vote, but by the statement's failure to correspond to objective reality. Therefore Christians, who historically have affirmed (whether implicitly or explicitly) the correspondence view of truth, argue that there are good historical and philosophical reasons to believe that the Christian revelation is objectively true. Any number of philosophical attacks have been leveled against the correspondence view of truth.[11] But the more subtle challenges come from ways of life that tend to erode this notion of truth, whether anyone has heard of the philosophical arguments or not. Many of these ways of life, it turns out, are perpetuated in cyberspace.

INFORMATION AND TRUTH

In chapter three we touched on the problem of information overload, but we must reflect further on how information relates to knowledge and wisdom. When we join the great network of cyberspace, an ocean of information is at our disposal (assuming we master the interface sufficiently). Our capacity to assimilate information profitably, however, is quite limited. French philosopher Jean Baudrillard puts it succinctly: "We live in a world where there is more and more information and less and less meaning."[12] Neil Postman expands on this: "The tie between information and human purpose has been severed, i.e., information appears indiscriminately, directed at no one in particular, in enormous volume and at high speeds, and disconnected from theory, meaning, or purpose."[13]

The recognition of meaning requires a manageable sensory and intellectual context in which one is neither overwhelmed by information nor lulled into inattention through understimulation. As Pascal noted, if we read too fast or too slow we miss the meaning.[14] Each soul has its optimal rate of ingestion, absorption, and digestion—a rate seldom in sync with the whirlwind velocities of technological culture.[15] Michael Heim warns that "when we pay attention to the significance of something, we cannot proceed at the computer's breakneck pace. We have to ponder, reflect, contemplate."[16] Jacques Ellul observes that an excess of information results in a "broken vision of the world" where information is never placed into an adequate historical or moral framework; therefore it makes no lasting imprint. "Excess of information goes hand in hand with a culture of forgetting. The mass of information produces a blind life with no possible roots or continuity."[17]

If we fail to attend to the meaning of a piece of information, we cannot accurately assess its truth. This is obvious in chat-room exchanges online. Each participant—and there can be as many as thirty—find on their screen a series of short messages from other participants. They can join in by typing their own message and sending it to the "room," which takes only a few seconds. As many as five or six exchanges between different participants may be happening at once. The combined messages scroll by at rapid rate, disappearing into nothingness. Given the rapidity of the exchanges, the evanescence of the text, and the multiplicity of topics, it is extremely difficult to find meaning in the utterances—let alone truth. These chat rooms are highly stimulating, diverting, and sometimes exciting (in a bizarre, cacophonous sense)—but they are not the best place to look for truth.

A column in the magazine *Virtual City* also illustrates the loss of meaning in cyberspace. The piece, called "Meaning in Life," begins somewhat seriously, with the author asking, "What's the point? Is this all there is?" He then recaps a click-by-click trek on the Internet, guided by a search engine that produced more than a hundred hits on the topic of "meaning of life." The sampling he lists is nothing more than a pastiche of the serious, the cynical, and the idiotic; it includes papal encyclicals, the *I Ching*, Monty Python, and a man who calls himself God. The conclusion: "Life's meanings, virtual or real, come as they come."[18] The meanings (plural) are haphazard, not hierarchical (Python and the Pope are equally citizens of the Net); they are optional, not necessary, because they "come as they come," rolling off the sea of data.

DIGITAL DIVERSIONS IN CYBERSPACE

However unsettling or even frightening cyberspace may become for those without roots in a sufficient worldview, for many it remains entrancing and ultimately diverting. In speaking of the human propensity for diversion, Pascal goes to great lengths to expose the varied diversions that prohibit people from seeking truth in matters of ultimate significance. In Pascal's day, diversion consisted of hunting, games, and other amusements. That repertoire of diversion is infinitesimal when compared with what is available in cyberspace— CD-ROM games, MUDs, MOOs, e-mail, chat rooms, and so on. Nevertheless, the human psychology of diversion remains the same, whatever the means of attainment. Pascal perceived that diversion consoles us in the face of our miseries; paradoxically, however, it becomes the worst of our miseries because it hinders us from thinking about our true condition "and leads us imperceptibly to destruction." If not for diversion, we would "be bored, and boredom would drive us to seek some more solid means of escape, but diversion passes our time and brings us imperceptibly to our death."[19]

Diversion serves to distract humans from a plight too terrible to stare in the face, namely, our mortality, finitude, and sinfulness. Pascal wants to unmask diversion for what it is—an attempt to escape reality, and an indication of something unstable and strange in the human condition. Interest in, and even addiction to, the entertaining is not simply silly or frivolous for Pascal, but reveals a moral and spiritual malaise begging for an explanation. The human condition is "inconstancy, boredom, anxiety."[20] We face an incorrigible mortality that delusively drives us to overcome the inevitable by means of the impossible: finding satisfaction and release through empty amusements that masquerade as worthwhile.

> Man is obviously made for thinking. Therein lies all his dignity and his merit; and his whole duty is to think as he ought. Now the order of thought is to begin with ourselves, and with our author and our end.
>
> Now what does the world think about? Never about that, but about dancing, playing the lute, singing, writing verse, tilting at the ring, etc. and fighting, becoming king, without thinking what it means to be a king or to be a man.[21]

Or, we may add, people think about more powerful tools for surfing the Net, faster modems, bigger and more colorful screens, more memory, more special effects, and so forth. The denizens of cyberspace seldom rest content with the status quo. Pascal notes that "if man were [naturally] happy, the less he were diverted the happier he would be, like the saints and God."[22] Diversion cannot bring sustained happiness, since it locates the source of happiness outside of us; thus, our happiness is dependent on factors often beyond our control, so that we are "liable to be disturbed by a thousand and one accidents, which inevitably cause distress."[23] No matter how sophisticated the computer system may be, bugs, viruses, worms, power surges, and ignorance still haunt the operations. Furthermore, the power can go out unexpectedly and the Internet bill can get out of control.

Diversions would not be blameworthy if they were recognized as such: trivial or otherwise distracting activities occasionally engaged in to avoid the harsh and unhappy realities of human life. But self-deception also comes into play. In the end "we run heedlessly into the abyss after putting something in front of us to stop us seeing it."[24] According to Pascal, this condition illustrates the corruption of human nature. "If our condition were truly happy we should feel no need to divert ourselves from thinking about it."[25] As T. S. Eliot put it, "Humankind cannot bear very much reality."[26]

Pascal says "there was once in man a true happiness, of which all that now remains is the empty print and trace," which he "tries in vain to fill with everything around him, seeking in things that are not there the help he cannot find in those that are." This, however, is futile because an "infinite abyss can be filled only with an infinite and immutable object; in other words by God himself."[27] "Grace fills empty spaces," according to Simone Weil, "but it can only enter where there is a void to receive it, and it is grace itself which makes this void."[28] Ecclesiastes adds that God has put eternity into the human heart, yet in such a way that we cannot make sense of it all or find peace without God's revelation and redemption.[29]

The compulsive search for diversion is often an attempt to escape the wretchedness of life. We have great difficulty being quiet in our rooms. Souls adrift from Christ are restless; they seek solace in cyberspace instead of satisfaction in truth. As Pascal said, "Our nature consists in movement; absolute rest is death."[30]

Many of today's interactive computer games divert millions of users through simulations of extreme violence and cruelty. Because even high-tech diversions can lead to boredom, the video stimulations and simulations must become increasingly sensational.[31] Games supposedly for children, such as Mortal Kombat and Night Trap, trade on electrocutions, decapitations, hearts ripped out of living opponents by martial art combatants, immolation, and sorority girls strung up on meat hooks.[32] In Mortal Kombat, the most popular video game of 1993, characters "vicariously bloody each other on the screen" in photorealistic fashion.[33]

Advertisements for 1995's most popular video game, Doom, read: "NOW THERE'S A PLACE MORE VIOLENT THAN EARTH."[34] One dedicated player of Doom confessed to one of the creators of the game that "Doom is my life."[35] It might just be a doomed life.

This is a serious matter. Social critic Allucquere Rosanne Stone claims that

> Within a short time, the number of hours that a broad segment of children will spend playing computer-based games will exceed the number of hours that they spend watching television. It is entirely possible that computer-based games will turn out to be the major unacknowledged source of socialization and education in industrialized societies before the 1990s have run their course.[36]

Of course, not all of these games are pernicious, but one whose imagination is contaminated by the images of violent and bizarre computer games cannot be directed by a holy God. As Pascal said, "Imagination magnifies small objects with fantastic exaggeration until they fill our souls, and with bold insolence cuts down great things to its own size, as when speaking of God."[37]

Cyberspace diversions often magnify nonexistent objects on colorful video screens, combine them with audio effects, and render them "interactive," thus filling our souls with unrealities while the reality of God is ignored or trivialized. For instance, a CD-ROM interactive game called "Afterlife" advertises itself as "the first world-building simulation that lets you manage two planes of 'unreal estate'—heaven and hell—simultaneously." The stupendous spiritual realities of eternal life and eternal death are simulated and trivialized for entertainment purposes. Nevertheless, it is still true that "between us and heaven and hell there is only this life, the most fragile thing in the world."[38] This fragility should drive us to our knees, not to exotic and irreverent simulations in cyberspace.

Cyberspace may be the greatest temptation yet offered to humanity to lose its soul in diversion. Having the senses inundated with information or overwhelmed with stimulation is not conducive to a soul finding serenity in the knowledge of the truth.

DATA, INFORMATION, AND KNOWLEDGE

Although the words are often used interchangeably in and around cyberspace, there is a world of difference between data, information, and knowledge. And the concept of wisdom is often avoided entirely in discussions of cyberspace. Futurists Alvin and Heidi Toffler wax ecstatic over the protean potential of the Third Wave, or information revolution, which is driven predominately by computer networks:

> We are interrelating *data* in more ways, giving them context and thus forming them into *information*; and we are assembling chunks of *information* into larger and larger models and architectures of *knowledge*.[39]

Although the Tofflers do not use *data, information,* and *knowledge* in a strictly synonymous way, they fail to distinguish them adequately. An increase in available data produces increased information, but discerning truth from error requires more than assembling gigantic models of purported knowledge. Not everything that greets the soul can offer it nourishment. Discernment is demanded. To aid in discernment, we will first define some terms.

Digital data normally refers to the storage and transmission of electronic units that can be translated into the symbols of human language. Although data and information are often used interchangeably,[40] distinguishing them clarifies two levels of technology.[41] The binary bits of cyberspace are not really information until they are converted into an understandable form. This is all too evident when I download a file that is incompatible with my software. I am greeted by a magnificent array of meaningless hieroglyphics—data trash.

Digital data are quantitative and reductive. The same amount of data is contained in the following three sentences:

1. Worship Jesus and live.
2. Worship Satan and live.
3. Worship Allah and live.

Digitally, these statements are equals (having the same number of letters), since the semantic dimension does not register in the quantification of data. Qualitatively, however, they are unequal with respect to truth and meaning. Eric Ness puts it well:

To travel on your computer, everything textual [and graphical] is increasingly broken into digital bits of data. . . . In this bit form your modem and your computer can't differentiate between the Bible, Cervantes or the Playmate of the Month. In our emerging information economy, they can all be bought and sold in metered forms, as if they were water or electricity. The Miss October centerfold may run you about the same connect time as the New Testament.[42]

Information refers to the linguistic or graphical material that can be understood by human perceivers. This book is information, although its contents can be stored as digital data. Information informs us; that is, it impresses our consciousness with its claims. It enters the soul through the senses and leaves some kind of mark or trace. Information, however, may or may not be *true*. If truth is the final refuge of the soul and its source of strength and stability, the acquiring of information is not spiritually sufficient.

Aleksandr Solzhenitsyn, a hero who, under Communism, suffered greatly for the truth, spoke at Harvard in 1978 of the "forfeited right of people *not to know*, not to have their divine souls stuffed with gossip, nonsense, vain talk. A person who works and leads a meaningful life has no need for this excessive and burdening flow of information"; indeed, "hastiness and superficiality" are the "psychic diseases of the twentieth century."[43] One must be able to separate the true from the false, to determine which pieces of information correspond to reality and which do not. For this reason Paul warned Timothy to "turn away from godless chatter and the opposing ideas of what is falsely called knowledge."[44]

True information, when comprehended as such, is *knowledge*. Knowledge is what we know to be true through the proper stewardship of our senses and exercise of our reason. As Pascal pointed out, knowledge is often hard-won and easily lost in a world of falsehood. Opportunities for error are legion. Some who suffer from information exhaustion never move on to knowledge because they deem knowledge of the truth to be impossible. An infinity of interconnected pieces of information may emerge from the data, linking us to the electronic hive; but knowledge, the awareness of truth, tends to disappear.

THE UNREAL HYPERREAL

Jean Baudrillard, a postmodern nihilist, speaks of the futility of mere information (which he refers to as "knowledge"):

> Excess knowledge is dispersed arbitrarily in every direction on the surface, but commutation is the only process to which it is subject. At the interfaces, interlocutors are connected up to one another after the fashion of an electronic plug in a socket. Communication 'occurs' by means of a sole instantaneous circuit, and for it to be 'good' communication it must take place fast—there is no time for silence. Silence is banished from our screens; it has no place in communication. Media images (and media texts resemble media images in every way) never fall silent: images and messages must follow upon the other without interruption.[45]

For Baudrillard, the constant bombardment of images and information does not indicate or mirror any objective reality. What comes on the screen—whether computer, television or movie—is not a representational map of an external reality, but a self-enclosed appearance that has no correspondence beyond itself.

Baudrillard comments that instead of the map simulating or depicting a territory, the "map" takes on a life of its own. Simulation is now "the generation by models of a real without origin or reality: a hyperreal. The territory no longer precedes the map, nor does it survive it."[46] When the sign (whether in language or image) is severed from what it supposedly signifies, it becomes "hyperreal." Baudrillard believes this emptying of the sign came with the explosion of communication technologies. The electronic media in general and the computer in particular easily generate compelling unrealities that, for all their psychological effect or economic consequence, fail to refer to anything at all. Signs no longer imitate or duplicate or even parody the real, but simply substitute for the real.[47] As mentioned in chapter one, when Avram went online as "Allison" and engaged in a lesbian affair with "Janine" in a MOO, the textual interaction between the two had no reference to reality. They inhabited a hyperreal environment as hyperreal agents, however passionately involved.

Baudrillard's remarks should not be taken as logical points that refute the correspondence view of truth; they are sociological and psychological observations that explain why it can be troublesome to seek truth by means of the electronic media. Because a hyperreality fails to correspond to anything outside of itself, it should be deemed a false representation of objective reality. Although there is an Avram playing the part of Allison, there is no Allison per se. The statement "Allison exists" refers to a hyperreality but is, according to the correspondence view of truth, actually false.

Baudrillard responds to the incorrigible system of hyperrealities by attempting to make peace with it because he accepts nothing that transcends it or relativizes it. For Baudrillard, God is dead, meaning is dead, truth is dead; and this emancipates us from any duty to match our ideas to objective reality and from any anxiety over failing at the attempt.[48]

Our answer to Baudrillard must conserve his insight that truth is simulated or counterfeited routinely in our "information age," not least of all in cyberspace; but we must also challenge his acquiescence to a truthless world. Although Baudrillard says that everything has become hyperreal and that truth has vanished as a category of thought, his own words about hyperrealities and the deceptions of electronic media cannot themselves by hyperreal. Otherwise there would be no reason to take his words seriously, as accurately describing the way things are. Technologies affect our sensibilities, often deadening them to truth, but technologies have not destroyed objective reality or the possibility of knowing it.

WISDOM AND WORLDVIEW

Even beyond combing information for knowledge, any sane use of knowledge requires *wisdom*, which is not merely the accumulation of facts. Social critic Theodore Roszak speaks of those who "lose their intellectual way in a forest of facts."[49] In the words of T. S. Eliot from "The Rock":

> Where is the Life we have lost in the living?
> Where is the wisdom we have lost in knowledge?
> Where is the knowledge we have lost in information?

Although a scarcity of information is at the root of many problems, such as the medical crisis of the Chinese student discussed in chapter three, many chronic maladies actually have little to do with the need for more information. Postman concludes that "there are very few political, social, and especially personal problems that arise because of insufficient information."[50] What we lack is wisdom.

Facts found in cyberspace and strung together will probably lack the imprint of wisdom, a faculty by which we rank the significance and meaning of what we know, discern what we need to know, and decide how to put what we know into action responsibly. Wisdom takes knowledge and discerns the meaning therein. Wisdom is truth applied to the soul as guided by divine love. Paul warns that "knowledge puffs up, but love builds up."[51] Living out truth in love is what makes a person wise, not the mere accumulation of knowledge or information.[52]

The mightiest hard drive, the fastest modem, the most sophisticated word processor, and the most powerful Internet search engine on the planet will not download wisdom into the human soul. The possession of wisdom is a uniquely personal quality not reducible to any technique. As computer analyst Stephen Talbot wisely says, "Human life can be sustained only within a sea of meaning, not a network of information."[53] Cyberspace is a matrix for highly mobile information—some true, some false; some helpful, some harmful; some profound, some trivial.

Postman argues that when established religious worldviews lose their compelling and binding power, "confusion inevitably follows about what to attend to and how to assign it significance."[54] Although Postman does not endorse a religious worldview, he recognizes the confusion that the secular situation affords. He speaks of our culture as a "technopoly," in which "available theories do not offer guidance about what is acceptable information in the moral domain."[55] In place of moral decisions we are left with merely practical ones. What *works* replaces what is *right*. Consequently, wisdom wanes. Postman, an unbeliever, nevertheless sees that the Bible functions as a "control mechanism" with respect to how we handle information:

> The Bible gives manifold instructions on what one must do and not do, as well as guidance on what language to avoid (on pain of committing blasphemy), what ideas to avoid (on pain of committing heresy), what symbols to avoid (on pain of committing idolatry).[56]

Unless we possess a robust worldview sufficient to sort and rank the barrage of information, we will be left with what Sven Birkerts calls a merely "lateral consciousness," lacking the vertical dimension of seeing life *sub specie aeternitus*, under the aspect of eternity. He claims that to see through data to the underlying patterns and laws, "one must have something to see through *to*. One must believe in the possibility of a comprehensive whole."[57]

Ironically, Birkerts fails to say what that "comprehensive whole" might be. He simply asserts that it—whatever it is—is necessary if we are to find a dimension of meaning capable of bringing order, insight, and wisdom to the vast expanses of networked information. He insists that the lateral consciousness of connection without transcendence is a menace to the very meaning of culture, the pursuit of truth, and the health of our souls. Although he laments the loss of the depth originally derived from "the Judeo-Christian premise of unfathomable mystery,"[58] he does not delve into that depth. However brilliant his analysis often is, Birkerts endeavors to win back meaning, truth, depth, purpose, and mystery from the claws of cyberspace with only a postdated check for unspecified funds in no known currency. He attempts to discipline the immensity of cyberspace—and the electronic media in general—with an empty category.

Birkerts does not speak of the soul in the religious sense of our immortal essence but rather in the "secular" sense of "inwardness . . . , that awareness we carry of ourselves as mysterious creatures at large in the universe." The soul "smelts meaning and tries to derive a sense of purpose from experience."[59] This functional description fails to sound out the soul as a substantial reality in need of a larger truth by which to orient itself, direct its energies, discipline its desires, free it from self-destruction, and teach it how and what to worship. While Birkerts points out the need for a vertical dimension to give meaning to the lateral, he describes the soul vaguely as "our orientation toward the unknown."[60] The unknown, however, will not elevate Birkerts or anyone above the electronic horizon of the network, the circuit, and the hive. It is from the Christian tradition that Birkerts derives much of the resources for his critique, yet he refrains from endorsing Christianity as true.

Similarly, Postman is a perceptive critic of technology, yet he fails to articulate the kind of worldview that is required if we are to sort out the vast amounts of information thrown at us. Although he seems to respect faith traditions (while also subjecting them to criticism), Postman denies that any "absolute knowledge" is possible (thus ruling out revelation)[61] and gives a strange argument that contradictory assertions can both be true if held side by side.[62] But vague and uncertain beliefs do not bring meaning, truth, or wisdom, nor do they offer an adequate "control mechanism" for sorting out information. Moreover, if both A and non-A can be true, then knowledge is impossible because we lack the most fundamental test for truth. Anything goes.[63]

WISDOM FROM ABOVE: BEYOND CYBERSPACE

The Christian tradition that both Postman and Birkerts recognize as historically significant claims that we can orient our souls toward truth because the Incarnation has made God known to human flesh.[64] It affirms that God is consistent and will not contradict himself.[65] It also proclaims that wisdom has been revealed through Jesus Christ.[66] Moreover, this wisdom is available to the seeker: "If any of you lacks wisdom, he should ask God, who gives generously to all without finding fault, and it will be given to him."[67]

For the Christian the vertical dimension is no mere concept but a living reality, for God descended to the horizontal dimension through Christ, "who, being in very nature God, did not consider equality with God something to be grasped, but made himself nothing, taking the very nature of a servant, being made in human likeness."[68] Christ's servanthood translates into our wisdom and understanding because God has "spoken to us by his Son, whom he appointed heir of all things."[69] The same God who spoke in person through Christ also speaks wisdom from above through his written word, as the author of Hebrews explains:

> For the word of God is living and active. Sharper than any double-edged sword, it penetrates even to dividing soul and spirit, joints and marrow; it judges the thoughts and attitudes of the heart. Nothing in all creation is hidden from God's sight. Everything is uncovered and laid bare before the eyes of him to whom we must give account.[70]

Living before the all-knowing eyes of God and attending to his dynamic word is the only antidote to the loss of truth, the loss of meaning, and the hypnotic diversion offered in cyberspace. The soul can thrive only in atmospheres that are rich with truth, and truth will only be conveyed by those dedicated to its demands. As Weil has said, "There is no possible chance of satisfying a people's need of truth, unless men can be found for this purpose who love truth."[71]

6

CYBERSEX: EROTICISM WITHOUT BODIES

AMERICAN CULTURE AT THE END of the millennium is close to sexually insane. At a minimum, it is sexually profligate, confused, and unable to draw wise ethical boundaries around sexual practices or to stay within specified boundaries. Sexuality is taken as a right to be exercised according to one's preferences, not as a sacred trust to be governed with wisdom according to the soul's best interests. Restraint is the price of civilization, and we are casting off restraint. The sexual scene in America today exhibits the relentless logic of a venerable Latin phrase: *corruptio optimi pessima*: "there is nothing worse than the corruption of the best."[1] Put another way, the higher something is, the farther it can fall.

Sexual intimacy is rooted in God's good creation and was divinely established for the joyful union of a man and woman within a covenant of trust, fidelity, and love, and for the continuance of the human family. When sexual expression splits apart this providential framework, the splinters fly out in all directions, injuring soul, body, and society. Chesterton highlighted this.

> The moment sex ceases to be a servant it becomes a tyrant. There is something dangerous and disproportionate in its place in human nature, for whatever reason; and it does really need a special purification and dedication. The modern talk about sex being free like any other sense, about the body being beautiful like any tree or flower, is either a description of the Garden of Eden or a piece of bad psychology.[2]

SEX OUT OF CONTROL

Many today are sexually displaced, disoriented, even devastated—victims of a very bad psychology. The evidence of this sexual displacement litters the cultural landscape. Since 1960, births out of wedlock have skyrocketed by more than 400 percent.[3] Some estimate that by the year 2000, 40 percent of all births in America will be illegitimate.[4] Approximately thirty million human lives have been destroyed through abortion. One in four pregnancies is aborted in America today.[5] The divorce rate has more than doubled since 1960,[6] and the United States has the highest divorce rate on the planet.[7]

In the wake of widespread divorce, the percentage of single-parent families has increased three-fold since 1960.[8] The fraying of the family has crippled the souls of many children who come from broken homes. These children are more likely than children from stable homes to engage in self-destructive behaviors such as failing in school, becoming pregnant as teenagers, committing suicide, abusing drugs, and engaging in criminality.[9] A frightening wave of juvenile crime is expected only to get worse.[10] Sexually transmitted diseases are rampant. AIDS terrorizes the sexual scene with its death sentences, and people scramble for "safe sex" through technologies instead of moral restraint within established standards.

Into this maelstrom of sexual mismanagement is thrown the exotic potentialities of cyberspace. We have argued that cyberspace is a medium that shapes whatever messages invade our souls. It has great promise but also holds great (and often invisible) pitfalls. Disembodied existence in a digital world connects us with others but only by leaving our physicality behind the screen. Truth itself may become elusive in the digital domain when distractions overwhelm our senses and simulated realities eclipse reality itself. What happens when a sexually untethered culture enters this data-flow of cyberspace?

In a world estranged from Eden, sexuality often fails where it should flourish and intrudes where it should not. In cyberspace, sexuality presents itself without the details of actual bodies in spatial, visual, olfactory, and tactile proximity. In this we find an anomaly: the physical sexual desires must be digitally dematerialized and distributed in the quest to find a silicon surrogate for skin. What drives this new mode of disembodied sex?

SEX WITHOUT SKIN

First, as sexual intimacy is progressively separated from its covenantal responsibilities, it tends to degenerate into the quest for private erotic satisfaction, whatever the means. The orgasmatron of Woody Allen's futuristic spoof, "Sleeper," offered orgasm for the isolated individual in its virtual sex booth. This notion, claims Mark Dery, "lurks beneath the surface of cyberspace."[11] When Paul condemns those whose "god is their stomach," he has something very similar in mind.[12]

Second, when the demand for sexual stimulation escalates, the consequences of sexual promiscuity become increasingly severe. In a world of AIDS, venereal diseases, and unwanted pregnancies, the ultimate prophylactic may be disembodiment, where "dalliances [are] conducted in virtual worlds."[13] Our fragile flesh is not always the best mode for satisfying a boundless thirst for erotic gratification, since it is so subject to the corruptions of overindulgence. In cyberspace, lust finds several ways of transcending the body while trashing the soul.

Those trysting at "text-sex" contact each other by entering a variety of group "chat rooms" where the messages of various participants appear on screen along with the other "posts" that have accumulated. These chat rooms may have names such as "Romance Connection," "Naughty Negligees," "Gay Room," "Naughty Girls," or "Women Who Obey Women."[14] Although I have never darkened the screen of a text-sex room, one chat room I was involved in moved in that direction when I was attempting to defend the institution of monogamy in a fast-paced forum. After one gratuitously salacious message was posted, I fled. Who knows what followed after my speedy departure.

Because these rooms are policed by "guides" on some online services, those desiring more explicit eroticism find participants that strike their fancy by using a "private message" command, which allows a one-on-one, private interaction on screen. Text-sex can be as varied as the sensual imaginations and writing skills of the participants, with every aspect of real-world sexual contact being described textually on-screen. Dery describes a rendezvous where an "online prostitute" offered to have text-sex with someone if he would provide her (or was it him?) with a pirated copy of a computer game.[15] He also reports that some cybernauts augment their textual stimulations with their own private accompaniment and type with one hand.[16] To enhance the situation, the participants may download each others' photographs to aid their imaginative endeavors.[17] These images are supposedly of the participants, but who knows?

Such encounters are not limited to one-on-one situations. The virtual environments of MUDs and MOOs, discussed in chapter one, may be used as sexual playgrounds—or battlefields. "Increasingly, unbridled lust is intruding on the sword-and-sorcery scenarios of these Tolkienesque worlds," notes Dery.[18] These cyberfantasies often include "net.sleazing," which science writer Howard Rheingold describes as "the practice of aggressively soliciting mutual narrative stimulation"; it is "an unsavory but perennially popular behavior in MUDland."[19] He also claims that "there are MUDs in which outright orgiastic scenarios are the dominant reality," although this is not true for all of them.[20] But things get worse. Just as there are virtual prostitutes, there are virtual rapes. There may be a virtual crime wave.

VIRTUAL SEXUAL ABUSE

Sherry Turkle explains that virtual rape may occur when a MUD player devises a way to possess another character textually, thus becoming its online ventriloquist, as it were. Such a perpetrator is then the only one typing out messages for both his character and the one normally played by another person. The real-world player at the other end sits at the screen in amazement and then disgust when she finds her on-screen character submitting to sexual acts she neither instigated nor consented to have.[21] She has lost control of her online persona to another online persona who is a sexual predator. Feminist cultural critic Anne Balsamo claims that "the anonymity offered by the computer screen empowers anti-social behavior such as . . . MUD-rape (an unwanted, aggressive, sexual-textual encounter in a multi-user domain)."[22]

Things do not get much stranger than this—technologically created virtual environments, populated by artificial personae who devise ways to ravish each other, with or without the other's consent. Even more surreal—or hyperreal—are the discussions that attempt to sort all this out ethically. Turkle claims that "the issue of MUD rape and violence has become a focal point of conversation on discussion lists, bulletin boards, and newsgroups to which MUD players regularly post."[23] The argument concerns whether this activity is real enough to be wrong or hyperreal enough to be permissible, with disputants coming down hard on both sides. The same issue is raised concerning "virtual adultery." Is it really unfaithfulness? After all, nothing was touched; it was a game, however sexually charged. Wasn't it?

The unreality defense of cybersex is complicated by the confession of one online experiencer named Julian Dibbell:

> Netsex is possibly the headiest experience the very heady world of MUDs has to offer. Amid flurries of even the most cursorily described [sexual activity], the glands do engage, and often as throbbingly as they would in a real-life assignation—sometimes even more so, given the combined power of anonymity and textual suggestiveness to unshackle deep-seated fantasies.[24]

In an online interview, Turkle responded to a question about virtual adultery by saying that some couples find such extramarital experimentation to be natural because partners "continue to have a sexual curiosity about other people" and this "is kind of a harmless way to work that through." But other people feel betrayed because emotional closeness is so tied to language, which is what the online affair is all about. Turkle's advice rings of relativism: "This issue of cybersex is something that different couples really need to work out between them. Different people make very different decisions about it."[25] Given the present divorce rate, we may question the wisdom of her counsel.

Before rendering some less relativistic responses, we need to assess three more cybersex modalities: sex in virtual reality, online pornography, and pornographic CD-ROMs.

SEX IN VIRTUAL REALITY

The term *virtual reality* is sometimes used broadly to refer to any communication or experience pertaining to cyberspace. More specifically, it refers to the immersion of a person's senses into artificial environments through technological replacements for the normal operations of sense. One dons a helmet or head-mounted display equipped with two computer-driven screens, which give a three-dimensional effect. One can also wear data gloves that control one's navigation through the virtual world.

Virtual-reality technologies have a broad variety of possible applications—in medicine, scientific experimentation, and elsewhere—and the limits of simulation are not yet known. On the bright side, virtual-reality therapy has been used to help people suffering from certain phobias such as fear of heights.[26] It has not taken long, however, for cyberspace enthusiasts to consider the strictly erotic possibilities. One scene from the popular horror/science fiction movie *Lawnmower Man* sparked the imagination of many. Jobe, who went from dullard to genius through virtual-reality therapy and drug treatments, puts the technology to a more hedonistic use as he and his girlfriend jump into their data suits to experience disembodied but ecstatic hypersex. Dery describes the scene: "In cyberspace, they appear featureless, quicksilver creatures, their faces flowing together and oozing apart in a mystical communion that dissolves body boundaries."[27]

Howard Rheingold imagines a full-body "smart suit" that registers all the body's external responses, converts them to digital data, and transmits them through the phone lines where another smart-suited partner receives and in turn transmits her own sex-data.[28] Rheingold spells this out rather gleefully:

> Now, imagine plugging your whole sound-sight-touch telepresence system into the telephone network. You see a lifelike but totally artificial visual representation of your own body and of your partner's. Depending on what numbers you dial and which passwords you know and what you are willing to pay (or trade or do), you can find one partner, a dozen, a thousand, in various cyberspaces that are no farther than a telephone number.[29]

This scenario boggles the mind, but the idea behind it is to simulate accurately the response of each physically absent partner such that a new virtual environment is created. (This is an especially peculiar combination of virtual presence and literal absence, since so many perceptual functions are simulated.)

The virtual-reality sex just described aims at verisimilitude—being lifelike—whereby people simulate their actual physical bodies on the screen. In this model, there is no deception per se, only simulation. Cyberspace theorists, however, have already gone far beyond these as-yet-nonexistent cybersex technologies. Since each partner is not physically present with the other, deception is possible and cannot be ruled out. Who or what exactly is on the other end of cyberspace in the smart suit? Two levels of simulation come into play here, two removals from reality. The first simulation is the virtuality itself. The second is the impersonation of the supposed partner at the other end. The Book of Jude's image of the false teachers who are like trees "without fruit and uprooted—twice dead" comes to mind.[30]

Dery speculates that the simulations could be as wide-ranging as the erotic imagination. One's virtual appearance could be enhanced by removing years and adding sexual endowments. Beyond the cosmetic, participants could switch genders or even create new hybrid beings too perverse to describe.[31] Some envision virtual sex with virtual objects that have no personal identity but are objects of sexual attraction, such as the long-dead but photographically omnipresent Marilyn Monroe. These sexual specters would be worked up through computer generation using photos, recordings, and animation. The simulation would be projected into the sex-suit of those willing to engage in pseudointimacy with an erotic nonentity wearing a (virtual) human body. Call it a case of high-tech, no touch, and low life.

This is an example of hyperreality, to use Baudrillard's term, if there ever was one—all image and no referent. It may presage the possibilities of hyperreal sexual activity. Cultural critic Guy Ballard's prediction in a 1970 interview may capture the mentality of many:

> I believe that organic sex, body against body, skin against skin, is becoming no longer possible simply because if anything is to have any meaning for us it must take place in terms of the values and experiences of the media landscape.[32]

VIRTUAL VALERIE

The explosion of CD-ROM multimedia is providing another possibility for "interactive" sexual activities without personal relationship. Pornographic video clips, text, animation, and still shots are incorporated into environments that allow participants to set their own pace and orchestrate the goings-on by pointing and clicking through a variety of salacious scenarios. A best-selling CD-ROM in this genre is "Virtual Valerie," on the market since 1990. The interaction of this forum aims at seducing Valerie, which is virtually assured.[33]

Virtual Valerie has several competitors, including a character called Donna Matrix, a "21st century Pleasure Droid," who has been called "a cross between Madonna and Arnold Schwarzenegger."[34] Again, we find a double-removal from reality. The image of Donna Matrix is that of a nonhuman, a "droid" or android; this is a simulation of a simulation with no original. Baudrillard's "era of simulation" has arrived, accompanied by "a liquidation of all referentials." This "is no longer a question of imitation, nor duplication, nor even parody. It is a question of substituting the signs of the real for the real."[35]

Another advertisement pulls no erotic punches. It needs to be quoted to be believed (and condemned).

> Now You Can Have Your Own GIRLFRIEND™ . . . a sensual woman living in your computer! . . . You can watch her, talk to her, ask her questions, and relate to her. Over 100 actual VGA photographs allow you to see your girlfriend as you ask her to wear different outfits and guide her into different sexual activities. . . . She will remember your name, your likes and dislikes.[36]

Feminist critic Susan Coyle comments that "this is the 'artificial intelligence' version of the plastic blowup doll. A full relationship without having to involve another human being." Computers become "the soulless companions that women are unable to be—obedient and unquestioning."[37]

There is more than a trace of misogyny creating the market for such games. They offer a virtually perfect solution for the man who wants a woman with no mind and no life of her own. We should pity the men whose loneliness and desperation drive them to engage in sexual games of virtual relationship, but we should also denounce the debauchery of sexual "interaction" with no one at home.

PORNOGRAPHY GOES ONLINE

This brief tour of the cybersex possibilities brings a whole new technological meaning to Freud's notion of polymorphic perversity. Perversity can morph (to use a popular computer term) into any number of forms through the medium of cyberspace. By contrast, the simple transmission of pornographic images over the Internet may seem tame. But this (unlike virtual-reality sex) is already on the Net, provoking intense debate and triggering national legislation.

The cover of the July 3, 1995, issue of *Time* brought the issue of "cyberporn" into national view. A startled child about six years old is shown in front of a keyboard, his wide-eyed face eerily illuminated by the unseen screen. The article generated a firestorm of controversy, particularly concerning its mention of an eighteen-month study by Carnegie Mellon University claiming that 83.5 percent of the digitized images stored on Usenet newsgroups are pornographic and driven largely by a demand for images dealing with pedophilia, bestiality, sadomasochism, ad nauseum.[38] An article in the New York Times challenged the study, saying it was "a poorly designed survey whose main conclusion . . . could not be supported by the research methods employed."[39] Others have also challenged it.[40]

Whatever the percentage of pornographic images might be, it is no surprise that our sex-crazed culture traffics in online pornography. Wired magazine reports that of "the 10 most accessed links from the Whole Internet Catalog's GNN Select," seven are sexual in nature.[41] A recent issue of Internet Underground prominently features advertisements for sexually charged Web pages where one can watch live strip shows, "access fetish films," and interact with top "adult stars."[42] Another site hawks such items as "hot pictures" and the "history of erotica."[43]

Regardless of how prevalent online pornography may be, its acquisition is far simpler than in precyberspace days when voyeurs had to obtain material from pornographic stores located in plain view in the real world. The fear of being exposed almost disappears when the material is available on screen. These cyberporn sites are supposedly for "adults only," but given the anonymity and deceptive possibilities of cyberspace, enterprising youths can and do make their way in.

This ease of access was sadly highlighted by the pseudonymous confessions of "the Flogmaster" in Internet Underground. This man rejoiced in the opportunities cyberspace afforded him to engage in sadomasochistic (the word was never used, of course) fantasies: "After years of guilty hiding I was now part of an anonymous society openly sharing interests and secrets that could not be expressed in any other forum."[44] Notice the strange wording he uses: "an anonymous society" that "shares." This poor soul is relieved that he can freely indulge his perverse desires without guilt; yet the only "society" in which it can be done must be anonymous. Self-deception drops to new depths, thanks to the online "community."

Political debates rage over whether the distribution of erotic material should be criminalized. As of this writing, the Telecommunications Act of 1996, which banned the distribution of indecent materials to minors, has been challenged in court as violating the First Amendment. Cyberlibertarians want unrestricted "free speech" online, while others argue that pornography is dangerous and should be controlled. Whatever the fate of the Telecommunications Act, cyberpornographers have, at times, been caught and prosecuted under existing laws. Robert Thomas, operator of the Amateur Action Bulletin Board Service in Milpitas, California, was convicted of sending images of women having sex with animals across the Internet to paying customers. Pulling in $800,000 in 1994, Thompson and his wife sold pornographic images from his stock of twenty-five thousand kinky photos. He was sentenced to three years in prison—presumably without benefit of a modem.[45] Thompson is hoping, though, that his case will make it to the Supreme Court.

In her newspaper column, Arianna Huffington rightly argues that the problem goes "far beyond indecency—and descends into barbarism," because the indecent images offered in cyberspace include depictions of child molestation, bestiality, sadomasochism, and how to find sexual enjoyment by killing children.[46] Even if prudent restrictions on cyberpornography were in place (which I favor), they might be difficult to enforce. Nevertheless, such prohibitions would make an important statement for decency.

Because it is unlikely that cyberspace will police itself very effectively, we need to find gatekeepers for ourselves and our families. There are technologies available to protect children from inappropriate material—programs such as Cybersitter, Surfwatch, Net Nanny, and Cyber Patrol. Of course, a computer program cannot be trusted to do the work of responsible parenting. Children need to internalize a worldview and a set of sensibilities that will become an inner gyroscope to keep them on course, whatever temptations they face. This is learned primarily through face-to-face interaction with parents and other family members. Nevertheless, part of loving one's children involves protecting them from harmful influences before they are mature enough to make wise decisions themselves.

WHAT CYBERSEX SAYS ABOUT THE SOUL

The cultural meaning of cybersex must be understood if we are to have any hope of addressing the tidal waves of change. Cybersex in its many forms ironically combines a Gnostic lust for disembodiment with a very earthy immersion in the flesh. Physical appetites seek gratification unencumbered by the drag of the physical body. Cybersex thus combines two defining aspects of pagan spirituality: the desire to transcend the material creation through mystical experience and the worship of sexual energies. This unstable alliance between the rejection of the body and the deification of erotic urges puts cybersex enthusiasts into a hopelessly conflicted dynamic. To use biblical language they "worshiped and served created things rather than the Creator"[47] while depreciating the physical world.[48]

By exalting one aspect of creation—the sex drive—and severing it from the rest of reality and God himself, people end up debasing what they seek to worship. This is the perennial pattern of all idolatry: the simulated gods are not divine and are thus powerless to fulfill the deepest spiritual desires of their benighted creators. The prophet Jeremiah knew it all too well: "Do men make their own gods? Yes, but they are not gods!"[49] "They followed worthless idols and became worthless themselves."[50] Although the technologies change, the impetus of idolatry remains constant.

If our culture's sexual practices are already out of control, catapulting them into cyberspace will hardly bring order and prudence to the situation. Instead of learning to live responsibly as embodied persons with sexual identities, cyberspace beckons us to experiment in an artificial world of stimulation, simulation, and seduction. Cybersex is the erotic equivalent of playing "air guitar"—plenty of motion, passion, and pretense . . . but no music.

Michael Heim observes that "the computer network simply brackets the physical presence of the participants, by either omitting or simulating corporeal immediacy." The "stand-in body reveals only as much of ourselves as we mentally want to reveal." It "lacks the vulnerability and fragility of our primary identity. The stand-in self can never fully represent us. The more we mistake the cyberbodies for ourselves, the more the machine twists ourselves into the prostheses we are wearing."[51]

Heim's observation applies directly to the sexual posturings we have discussed. There is a disorientation of one's identity through becoming "the prostheses we are wearing." Sexual identities assumed online may easily work their way into the real world. Those who dismiss online sexual activity as merely "a game" fail to take this seriously. Our thoughts shape our behavior, and an overstimulated imagination is a powerful impetus in everyday life. The imagination, like every one of our faculties, must be disciplined and directed by the good, the true, and the beautiful. This is especially crucial in the sexual dimension, where governance of one's thoughts is an integral aspect of wisdom.

This criticism does not apply to the responsible use of e-mail, chat rooms, or bulletin boards to initiate relationships that do not terminate at the terminal or become reckless. One hears stories of people who connected (I can not bring myself to say "met") online, developed a more in-depth, written relationship, and finally met face-to-face for romantic purposes. In these cases, cyberspace is not a substitute for full-blooded and embodied real life, but contributes to it.

Just as romance has been cultivated through letters, so can it be pursued legitimately through cyberspace as well—as long as virtuality does not replace and usurp reality. For those who are awkward or shy in person, textual exchange online might serve as a warm-up for an embodied encounter. *Time* reports that a reserved man named Dave Marsh spent four years communicating online with a woman named Audrey. He says, "Even though I'm the most private person you'd ever want to meet, I let my guard down right away [online]." In 1993, two years after meeting Audrey face-to-face, the two married.[52]

SEXUALITY: THE YES AND NO OF THE GOSPEL

In a category entirely different from cyberspace "pen pals" are cases of "virtual rape," "virtual adultery," "virtual prostitution," and so forth. The wrongness of these activities is plain if we heed Jesus' words: "You have heard that it was said, 'Do not commit adultery.' But I tell you that anyone who looks at a woman lustfully has already committed adultery with her in his heart."[53] The disembodied sexual exchange practiced in cyberspace is even closer to physical sex than the activity of the solitary imagination described by Jesus. Our sensory field is more fully occupied and engaged and (at least in some cases) another person is actively involved, even if not present in body. Furthermore, one might indulge illicit sexual predilections in the anonymity of cyberspace that one would be hesitant to act on in real life. This could serve as a bridge to more embodied immorality down the road.[54]

The essence of freedom, according to Christ, is the consecration of the entire self—heart, soul, and mind—to the love of God.[55] The titillating exploration of sexual fantasies (in cyberspace or otherwise) fails to honor God; it dissipates energies meant for other purposes. The imagination, when undisciplined, can become a tyrannical ruler, overwhelming restraint. This is why Pascal called it "the master of error and falsehood."[56] James amplifies the principle of guarding the imagination: "Each one is tempted when, by his own evil desire, he is dragged away and enticed. Then, after desire has conceived, it gives birth to sin; and sin, when it is full-grown, gives birth to death."[57]

Paul has very much the same idea in mind when he presents himself as one who takes "captive every thought to make it obedient to Christ."[58] In a justly famous passage on the stewardship of our awareness, Paul exhorts us to attend earnestly to matters of objective value:

> Finally, beloved, whatever is true, whatever is honorable, whatever is just, whatever is pure, whatever is pleasing, whatever is commendable, if there is any excellence and if there is anything worthy of praise, think about these things. Keep on doing the things that you have learned and received and heard and seen in me, and the God of peace will be with you.[59]

The peace of God from the God of peace is promised to those who guard their minds from sensual immorality and focus instead on things worthy of sustained attention. In Proverbs we are exhorted, "Above all else, guard your heart, for it is the wellspring of life."[60] David confessed, "I will set before my eyes no vile thing."[61] In following David's example we may need to enact measures against our being led into temptation, given the ease of access to perverse material. One student of mine, for example, was asked by his friend to install a computer program that would block any pornographic material because of his weakness in this area. He was following the biblical command to "flee temptation," as we should as well, whether or not we suffer from his particular weakness.

Because we all have the propensity to sin and give in to the manifold temptations to "love the world or the things in the world,"[62] we must learn to say "No" with authority, recognizing God as the Author of life and sexuality but not the author of sin. As Paul said to his friend Titus: "For the grace of God that brings salvation has appeared to all people. It teaches us to say 'No' to ungodliness and worldly passions, and to live self-controlled, upright and godly lives in this present age."[63]

The "No" of gospel obedience always presupposes the deeper "Yes" of Jesus Christ himself: "For no matter how many promises God has made, they are 'Yes' in Christ. And so through him the 'Amen' is spoken by us to the glory of God."[64] E. Stanley Jones, a prolific author and effective missionary to the East, understood this well: "Christianity means to say Yes to [Jesus'] Yes. Surrender to his will and you will be saying Yes to his Yes. The whole universe is behind it. You will walk the earth a conqueror, afraid of nothing."[65]

The Yes to God is a Yes to being one-flesh with one partner, a Yes to heterosexual exclusivity, and a Yes to fidelity. Within the echo chamber of these resounding affirmations, their corresponding denials become both possible and desirable. Reflecting on his own long marriage, Jacques Ellul testifies in this way:

> I believe that throughout life, in spite of descents and setbacks, only one love resists the wasting of time and the diversity of our desires. How poor and unhappy are those who have not been able to grasp it or live it out. . . . Love of a single person is marvelously exclusive. This is the point of God's statement . . . "I am a jealous God" (Exod. 20:5)—not through weakness or in the sense of human jealousy, but because of his fullness which includes all things in itself.[66]

The hyperrealities of cybersex may seem heavenly in a twisted techno-Gnostic sense (at least for a time), yet, because they are detached from God's ethical pattern for his creatures they are much more akin to hell. Simone Weil put it this way in a suggestive fragment: "Two conceptions of hell: the ordinary one (suffering without consolation); mine (false beatitude, mistakenly thinking oneself to be in paradise)."[66] Both conceptions of hell are true. Hell may begin with earth's errant ecstasies (digital or otherwise), but it does not end there for the unrepentant. One may gain much of what this cursed planet has to offer and lose one's soul in the transaction. Jesus' unanswerable question should reverberate throughout all of cyberspace:

> For those who want to save their life will lose it, and those who lose their life for my sake will find it. For what will it profit them if they gain the whole world but forfeit their life? Or what will they give in return for their life?[68]

7

❧❧❧

TECHNOSHAMANISM: DIGITAL DEITIES

TIMOTHY LEARY IS DEAD, but he lives on in cyberspace. On the Internet, the Timothy Leary home page explains: "Just after midnight, in his favorite bed among loving friends, Timothy Leary peacefully passed on. His lasts words were 'why not?' and 'yeah.' " Leary, who had been terminally ill for several months, had considered committing suicide via a live feed through the Web. It was not to be, but Leary kept visitors to his site informed on his declining condition and philosophized freely about it, claiming he had no fear of death. He announced in 1995 that he was "thrilled" to learn he had terminal prostate cancer and remarked that "how you die is the most important thing you ever do. It's the exit."[1] Leary died a "designer death," as he put it, displayed in cyberspace for all to access.

TIMOTHY LEARY AND GENERATION X

The psychedelic savant of the counterculture, although well past the salad days of extensive public exposure, had continued to stir up controversy and hold the fringe in thrall. In recent years, his emphasis moved from hallucinogenic drugs (which he never renounced) to the mind-expanding possibilities of cyberspace. The *New York Times* reported that in the weeks before his death, Leary handled many interviews in order "to market his estate and its provision for the maintenance of his [Internet] Web site."[2] I reached his Web site to find it laid out as his home, with a library, cyberroom, and updated reports on his health. When I checked the latter room, I read, "Timothy has passed. Pulse=0. Blood Pressure=0/0. But Tim says he's feeling great."

Although in his seventies, Leary, ever the provocateur, attracted the attention not only of aging Grateful Deadheads, but those of Generation X as well. His fame spread to both hippies and hackers (and the overlap between the two). Leary features prominently in Generation Xer's Douglas Rushkoff's offbeat manifesto, *Cyberia: Life in the Trenches of Hyperspace.*[3] Rushkoff tells us that Cyberians (the younger denizens of cyberspace) who use "drugs do not need to learn that reality is arbitrary and manipulable, or that the landscape of consciousness is broader than normal waking-state awareness suggests" because they have already learned these things from Leary and the psychedelic author and adventurer Ken Kesey.[4] Rushkoff eulogized Leary on Leary's home page, saying, "Tim's whole trip—from psychedelics to computers to designer dying—was to communicate the fact that people are capable of taking charge of their own brains, hearts, and spirits."[5]

Leary's later years were dedicated to leading the march into cyberspace, which he viewed as a zone for unlimited human potential. He believed that virtual-reality experiences and online communications could serve the same purposes as hallucinogenic drugs. Leary modified his famous credo of the 1960s, "Tune in, turn on, and drop out," to "Turn on, boot up, and jack in" and proclaimed that "PC [personal computing] is the LSD of the 1990s."[6] (It was not an either/or for Leary; in a 1995 interview in the online magazine *HotWired*, Leary admitted to having taken LSD three months earlier).[7]

Leary and Rushkoff go further to suggest that the 1960s psychedelic experimentation and interest in Eastern religions directly influenced the development of modern computers and cyberspace. According to Leary, Apple Computer cofounder Steve Jobs "went to India, took a lot of acid, [and] studied Buddhism," while Bill Gates, cofounder of Microsoft, "was a big psychedelic person at Harvard." Leary explains that "it makes perfect sense to me that if you activate your brain with psychedelic drugs, the only way you can describe it is electronically."[8] Rushkoff claims that "psychedelics are a given in Silicon Valley. They are as established as Intel, Stanford, marriage, or religion. The infrastructure has accommodated them."[9]

CYBERSPACE AND THE COUNTERCULTURE

The continuing popularity of Leary and the countercultural ethos is not just a retrotrend or a dip into hippie nostalgia. Many of those advocating the mind-expanding possibilities of cyberspace in one form or another are survivors from the sixties. Besides Leary, these include Stewart Brand, ex-hippie and editor of *The Whole Earth Catalogue*, and John Perry Barlow, lyricist for the Grateful Dead and an outspoken advocate of computer rights through the Electronic Frontiers Foundation, which he helped found.[10] Many of the beliefs and sensibilities of the counterculture have made their way through the seventies and eighties and into much of the cyberculture of the nineties.[11]

Although the political rebellion and spiritual experimentation of the sixties' counterculture tended to reject technology, with the exception of stereo sound systems and chemically synthesized drugs such as LSD, today's followers of the counterculture more commonly integrate and mystify new technologies into a nonmaterialistic and non-Christian worldview. Mark Dery summarizes the marriage of cyberspace technologies and the psychedelic orientation (cyberdelia) in this way: "Cyberdelia reconciles the transcendentalist impulses of sixties' counterculture with the infomania of the nineties. As well, it nods in passing to the seventies, from which it borrows the millenarian mysticism of the New Age."[12] Cyberspace critic Erik Davis makes this compelling connection:

> New Age elements are rife throughout the post-1960s' Bay Area culture that laid the groundwork for much of what we call cyberspace. A psychedelic, do-it-yourself spirituality directly feeds the more utopian elements of the Northern California subculture of Virtual Reality designers, computer artists, and computer programmers, whose forums include *The Whole Earth Review*, *Mondo 2000*, and the WELL (a Sausalito-based electronic bulletin board. . .). For many of these folks, computers are the latest and among the greatest tools available for the achievement of the Aquarian goal: the expansion of consciousness by whatever means necessary.[13]

This mystification of technology loomed large in Rushkoff's interview of Britt Welin, a follower of Terence McKenna. McKenna, heir-apparent of the Timothy Leary legacy, is prone to such metaphysically melodramatic utterances as, "I think every person who takes five or six grams of psilocybin mushrooms in silent darkness is probably on a par with Christ and Buddha, at least in terms of input."[14] Britt Welin is both an acid-head and a cybernaut, and sees no contradiction between the two. She and her like-minded spouse adopt the idea of "technoanimism" and "think of technology itself as an animistic dynamic that filters through the individual machines, being an over spirit to them—an animistic spirit that's way beyond what humans are comprehending on their own level."[15]

Britt claims that when "you tune into a cyberspace environment [while on psychedelic drugs], you lose your parameters and you find yourself entirely within the electronic environment."[16] Britt's husband Ken also strives for union with cyberspace. He says, "Our video-computer system's set up to ease us into a level of intimacy where we can use it in a transparent sense" and "enter into a trance relationship with it." It then "ends up having a spiritlike existence."[17]

Author Allucquere Stone describes an experience with computing in similarly mystical terms but without overt reference to hallucinogenic drugs. After she began writing programs for a computer that she found in a dumpster, she

> made this kind of intuitive symbolic connection to the machine. It was so intense. The wheels began to turn, I could see the planets moving and the atoms vibrating, and I could see mind with a capital M. I could reach down into the very soul of this thing. I could talk to it. It was this sense of, well, here was the physical machine and here was the virtual machine, the abstract machine. It was a living creature that I could reach into and feel the circuitry. I could feel what the code was like.[18]

Stone claims she is not alone in this experience of electronic enlightenment. She says that the "interactive potential of the machine has created a novel category of what I call *quasi guys.*"[19] According to Erik Davis, the labyrinthine recesses of cyberspace with its unfathomable complexities and strange potencies "may soon appear to be as strangely sentient as the caves, lakes, and forests in which the first magicians glimpsed the gods."[20] To the sacred and mysterious natural spaces of unwired ancient animists we may now add the sacred and mysterious cyberspaces of the wired modern animists. Leary and a co-writer wax ecstatic on the same theme, but invoke the ancient alchemist:

> Today digital alchemists have at their command tools of a precision and power unimagined by their predecessors. Computer screens ARE magical mirrors, presenting alternate reality at varying degrees on command (invocation).[21]

They see computers as fulfilling the goal of "magick" as defined by arch-occultist Aleister Crowley: "the art and science of causing change to occur in conformity with our will."[22]

THE NEW AGE DAWNS—AGAIN

The yearning for a New Age to spring from the divine depths of human consciousness is hardly new; it is an ancient aspiration, an occult orientation to the divine, the world, and the self that sees them all as part of one ultimate reality.[23] The new spin on the old view is the addition of cybertechnologies as essential aids in the process of self-discovery or even as the manifestation of the New Age itself. Some technovisionaries, such as John Perry Barlow, invoke the evolutionary scenario of French Jesuit thinker and paleontologist Teilhard de Chardin to ground their viewpoint.[24]

Teilhard saw evolution as the fundamental category for all existence. He used this model of reality, which he spiritualized to transcend naturalism, to reinterpret all the foundational doctrines and symbols of Christian faith. Instead of the literal second coming of Jesus at the end of the age, he predicted the emergence of the noosphere (or mind-sphere), a level of unified consciousness that would constitute, in essence, the divinizing of the entire planet. This "noogenesis" would culminate in the Omega Point, the end of history and climax of cosmic evolution.[25]

Teilhard died in obscurity in 1955, far before the cyberspace revolution; but various thinkers surmise that cyberspace may just be the noosphere he anticipated. Teilhard himself may have had some inkling of the technologies to come.[26] Barlow sees the eventual coming of a cosmic mind presaged even in something as pedestrian as e-mail:

> Watching e-mail messages come and go can give you a holy sense of mission. It's synaptic firing, across the web of a slowly evolving nervous system. In a couple of hundred years, every synapse on this planet will be continuously and seamlessly connected to every other synapse on the planet. One great wad of mind.[27]

For a time Marshall McLuhan saw communications technologies in general as laying the foundation for the noosphere, as an extension of the human nervous system;[28] later, however, he rejected this view in a letter to the philosopher Jacques Maritain. He wrote:

Electric information environments being utterly ethereal foster
the illusion of the world as spiritual substance. It is now a reasonable facsimile of the mystical body [of Christ], a blatant manifestation of the Anti-Christ. After all, the Prince of this world is a
very great electric engineer.[29]

More recently Jean Houston, a New Age consciousness
researcher and spiritual advisor,[30] said she frequently uses the Internet
to converse with Green parties around the world as well as to play the
fantasy role-playing game, Dungeons and Dragons. "It's an extraordinary confluence of consciousness. Teilhard's noosphere is alive and
well."[31] Unlike Barlow, she need not wait. It's here.

SHAMANS WITH MODEMS

This "extraordinary confluence of consciousness" in cyberspace may
or may not be identified with the noosphere, but a raft of technopagans are tapping into cyberspace as a realm for mystical discovery,
magical powers, and evolutionary advancement. The use of cyberspace for these ends is often called technoshamanism. Technoshamanism, in all its permutations, is more than the latest fad
from San Francisco—although a high concentration of such activity
is located there. Although it is not an organized movement, it represents a growing cultural trend to deify cyberspace. The tribal
shaman of ancient, pagan religions was a mediator between the spiritual and material worlds who experienced mystical ecstasies and initiated others into the same communion with higher powers.[32]
Technoshamanism eliminates the middleman—although it is not
without visionaries, philosophers, and programmers—and offers mystical connections in cyberspace to everyone with a modem. Anyone
can be a (techno)shaman.

In a perceptive article in the New Republic, Alexander Star
explains the outlook well: "For the current visionaries, virtual reality
and smart drugs enable the user to 'storm the reality studio' (in
William Burrough's words), overcome the mediations of language
and instantiate new realities at will."[33] The essence of technoshamanism may be summarized in this statement by a pagan practitioner, "May the astral plane be reborn in cyberspace."[34]

In an extensive article on technopagans, Erik Davis sees parallels between the notion of magic as "the science of the imagination, the art of engineering consciousness and discovering the virtual forces that connect the mind-body with the physical world," and "our dizzyingly digital environment of intelligent agents, visual databases, and online MUDs and MOOs."[35] Technopagans believe that these technologies can serve as occult sacraments in the digital age because technopagans "honor technology as part of the circle of human life, a life that for Pagans is already divine."[36]

Mark Pesce, a self-confessed technopagan, claims that both "cyberspace and magical space are purely manifest in the imagination. Both spaces are entirely constructed by your thoughts and beliefs."[37] The pantheism/animism/polytheism mix of technoshamanism is expressed when Pesce explains, "I think computers can be as sacred as we are, because they can embody our communication with each other and with the entities—the divine parts of ourselves—that we invoke in that space."[38] In his mind's eye, he pictures cyberspace as "the computer equivalent of holography, in which every part of a fragment represents the greater whole."[39] Pesce later found that this corresponds with the Eastern idea of the net of Indra, in which each jewel reflects every other jewel.[40] The Internet's ability to form a myriad of electronic connections seemed to him to reflect this idea. The analogy, however, is flawed, as every point in cyberspace does not connect with, let alone reflect, every other point. It is, nevertheless, an attempt (albeit a poor one) to invoke "transhuman powers . . . from the machine rendered transcendent through human guidance," in Birkerts's words.[41]

Technopagans are also attracted to the idea of cybersex and gender morphing. A woman named legba [sic], a witch, enjoys cybersex and morphing because "they can be intensely magical. It's a very, very easy way of shapechanging." Legba likens this to the traditional shamans, whom she says are "between genders, or doubly gendered." Moreover, "morphing and net.sex can have an intensity and unsettling effect on the psyche, one that enables the ecstatic state from which Pagan magic is done."[42]

Another pagan, Tyagi Nagasiva, has "cobbled together his own mythic structures, divination systems, and rituals—an eclectic spirituality well suited to the Net's culture of complex interaction."[43] Nagasiva engages in "chaos magic" in which participants do not rigidly follow the occult tradition but create their own rules or ignore them altogether, "spontaneously enacting rituals that break through fixed mental categories and evoke unknown—and often terrifying—entities and experiences."[44] He claims that most pagans go online to coordinate rituals in real life whereas chaos magicians say, "Let's do the ritual online."[45] Nagasiva inhabits this ritual space from four to six hours a day.

THE PROBLEM WITH DIGITAL DEITIES

Technoshamanism attempts to sacralize the silicon, to find mystery in the works that our hands have made. Because of the influence of strange and sometimes wonderful computer technologies, those not grounded in God's own revelation in Christ and the Scriptures will seek revelations as they can.[46] Apart from God, where better to search than in cyberspace? It is as close as the keyboard and as esoteric as the Internet. It can be as engrossing as any technology in existence. Its mysteries beckon exploration; its potentials are not fully known. Through its massive connectivity it offers a kind of *visio dei*, a God's-eye vision of endless data through the dimensions of cyberspace. This explains the aspiration of Jobe from the movie *Lawnmower Man*, who, having tasted the powers of computers, wanted to incorporate all knowledge into himself by becoming one with cyberspace. He would become, in his words, a "cyber-Christ" (although in the end he acted more akin to a cyber-Satan).

Heim rightly comments that

> Our love affair with computers, computer graphics, and computer networks runs deeper than aesthetic fascination and deeper than the play of the senses. We are searching for a home for the mind and heart. . . . The world rendered as pure information not only fascinates our eyes and minds, but also captures our hearts. We feel augmented and empowered. Our hearts beat in the machines.[47]

Of course, the same description can be given for any form of idolatry. As the Jewish philosopher Abraham Heschel commented, the existence of idols bears a perverse testimony to our need for the divine. If we will not accept the divine on its own terms, we will create fascinating and mystifying surrogates that take on a life of their own, with a seductive appeal that we cannot easily resist.[48]

The sacred grove seems tame compared to the technological wizardry of a pagan MOO or MUD. When we "turn on, log on, and jack in," we feel linked to a larger reality that transcends the finitude and frailty of our offline lives. Yet this reality is only virtual, the work of human minds and hands, however much it may absorb its practitioners into itself. It is a projection or extension of humanity, a medium for a myriad of messages. As such, it cannot grant final satisfaction to the soul.

PASCAL ON THE GOD BEYOND CYBERSPACE

A passage from Pascal enables us to understand the essential spiritual problem of technoshamanist spirituality.

> The Stoics say: "withdraw into yourself, that is where you will find peace." And that is not true. Others say, "Go outside: look for happiness in some diversion." And that is not true: we may fall sick. Happiness is neither outside us nor inside us; it is in God, both outside us and inside us.[49]

The lure of technoshamanism lies in its promise that the self will find its spiritual fulfillment in an artificial but deified environment of its own design. It thereby seeks liberation both inside and outside itself. It diverts itself from real life through cyberspatial arrangements, all the while withdrawing into an internalized world of the imagination. Yet neither the inbreaking or outgoing forces find a center of steadfast security. By withdrawing into oneself, one finds only oneself; and out of the heart, as Jesus said, emanates "evil thoughts, sexual immorality, theft, murder, adultery, greed, malice, deceit, lewdness, envy, slander, arrogance and folly."[50] Out of the self springs not salvation, but rather the evidence that salvation is needed. To invoke Pascal again: "It is vain that you seek within yourselves the cure of your miseries. All your intelligence can only bring you to realize that it is not within yourselves that you will find either truth or good."[51]

False philosophers in Pascal's day, as the technopagans of today, urged their hearers that they were not alienated from God, but that God was a handy idea with which to build up their own pride.

> The philosophers . . . do not know what your true good is, nor what your true state is.

How could they provide cures for your ills which they did not even know? Your chief maladies are the pride that withdraws you from God, and the concupiscence [lust] that binds you to the earth; all they have done is to keep at least one of these maladies going. If they gave you God for an object it was only to exercise your pride; they make you think that you were like him and of a similar nature.[52]

By looking outside to cyberspace, we find diversion galore but not guaranteed satisfaction (as we discussed in chapter five). We may fall sick and not be able to log on. The hard disk might crash. A computer virus or worm might infect and disable. The power might go out or lightning may hit the telephone lines. We might even be "virtually raped" or otherwise roughed up in a MOO or MUD.

Pascal claims that the answer lies neither in extroversion nor introspection but in God, who "is both outside us and inside us." Pascal's comment is fragmentary, but his meaning is clear from the Scriptures. God is the sole source of our truest blessedness, a beatitude unavailable elsewhere. God is outside of us because he is the Creator who transcends the universe that he made out of nothing. As the all-powerful Creator, God is not reducible to any aspect of creation; no idol can contain or express his power or goodness. Nevertheless, God is present at every point of this world. He upholds the universe through the Word of his power and nothing is hidden from his sight.[53]

Beyond this, God is redemptively present in those who abandon godless diversion and self-deification and embrace Christ's atoning death on the cross as their deliverance. Speaking to followers of Christ, Paul speaks of "Christ in you, the hope of glory."[54] God reveals his transcendence and immanence through the prophet Isaiah:

For this is what the high and lofty One says—he who lives forever, whose name is holy; I live in a high and holy place, but also with him who is contrite and lowly in spirit, to revive the spirit of the lowly and to revive the heart of the contrite.[55]

THE DANGERS OF MAGIC AND THE OCCULT

Magic, unlike revealed religion, has always sought initiation into a higher state of consciousness in order to manipulate reality through the acquisition of arcane powers. The practice of magic is one coping mechanism of fallen beings who perceive their insufficiency in a cursed world, yet who refuse to submit to either God's personal rule or fate's impersonal dominance. Magicians seek to create their own reality through spiritual technologies of all kinds—whether incantations, visualizations, rituals, or online environments. The goal is the attaining of power over an otherwise resistant reality that dooms us to degeneration, disease, and ultimately death. Magic attempts to undo the effects of the Fall apart from grace by attempting to conquer the effects of sin apart from the Savior. It seeks power from below, instead of grace from above.[56]

From a biblical perspective, such occult power-mongering (either online or offline) is nothing less than rebellion against the Creator and an invitation to the dark powers that masquerade as light— whether or not the magicians believe in Satan and demons. God's prohibition of magic and the occult flows from a jealous love of his creatures.[57] Since the eternal and uncreated God is the apex of all value, meaning, and excellence, any defection from his divine counsel results in alienation. Into this void rushes the counterfeit of a deified creation, pressed into a spiritual service it cannot discharge—the salvation of the soul. Given the spiritual impotence of the creation to save itself, the demonic world finds its opportunity to pose as divine, offering a "counterfeit infinity" in place of the true God.[58] Paul warned that "Satan himself masquerades as an angel of light"[59] and Jesus admonished us to remember that the devil is the father of lies.[60]

Although cyberspace technologies in themselves need not be demonic, their seductive simulations and compelling magnetism easily turn them into conduits of deception and distortion when appropriated by the pagan practitioner. Because such technologies facilitate the construction of artificial environments, they can be a particularly powerful tool in the hands of cybermagicians who long to "create their own reality" one way or another.

Earlier quotations from technopagans referred to unspecified "entities" contacted through cyberrituals. These do not describe human participants, but spiritual beings. Occultists through the centuries have used visualization, drugs, and meditation to contact creatures otherwise aloof and invisible. In light of the imaginative occult environs frequented by technopagans in cyberspace, it would be no surprise if this medium should attract less than angelic agents who, like opportunistic infections, will exploit any opening they can find.[61]

Rushkoff speaks of a technopagan named Green Fire who worries that his cyberspiritual adventures "could lead me to a place that I wouldn't want to be. It's like a puzzle or a maze and I could get lost." Green Fire warns, "Magic is a dangerous thing. There is a new age belief that you can never get hurt; that's not true. You can get hurt very bad."[62] This echoes the testimonies of many who have been burned by the occult. It is neither tame nor good.

UNMASKING THE PSYCHEDELIC CLAIMS

Leary and Rushkoff claim that some who have used hallucinogenic drugs have been inspired to create advanced computer technologies. They also believe that the combination of cyberspace exploration and the ongoing use of hallucinogens is crucial to awakening a higher consciousness that will be instrumental in bringing down the oppressive, dominant society and building a better one. This argument is more virtual than real for several reasons.

First, that some superstars such as Bill Gates and Steven Jobs may have used LSD and become technological innovators fails to establish either that LSD was the cause of their intellectual breakthroughs or that most people who ingest hallucinogenic drugs will have similar experiences. Gates and Jobs are both highly intelligent people who probably would have come up with their ideas with or without hallucinogens. In any event, it would be very difficult to prove that mind-altering drugs were the efficient cause of their success, although such claims make for hot sound bites. A visit to People's Park in Berkeley, California, will reveal any number of acid heads whose trips led them to homelessness and insanity and not to the forefront of cyberspace. Less tragic examples abound as well.

Second, even if we grant that the use of hallucinogenic drugs was instrumental in the computer revolution, this does not prove that the computer revolution is an unmitigated good or that the world-view generated by hallucinogenic drugs is true. I have argued throughout this book that the technologies created by the likes of Jobs and Gates are not cornucopias of pure blessing. They have a dark side that is all too often ignored in the bright lights of cyberculture.

Moreover, various experiences can produce beliefs that "work" or are "successful," yet do not truly correspond to reality.[63] Someone may believe that she misplaced five hundred dollars because of carelessness. She then reforms her life and becomes an affluent business-woman. The idea that she lost the money "worked" for her. As she learns later, however, the money was stolen, not misplaced. Her belief, then, was false, even if it was beneficial.[64] Similarly, a hallu-cinogenic experience might be credited for some discovery in com-puter technology, but this, in itself, does not establish the truth of monism, pantheism, animism, or polytheism—worldviews that often (but not always) come through these experiences.

We should consider a key difference in terminology. Although technopagans prefer the word *psychedelic*, the term *hallucinogenic* is more appropriate. A hallucinogen is a drug that induces a halluci-nation, an essentially deceptive experience that seems very real. The assumption behind this term is that our normal thought processes and sensory capacities are better guides to objective reality than a chemically induced experience, because the artificially altered mind is not necessarily the illuminated mind. A so-called psychedelic drug, on the other hand, intensifies sensory perception, ostensibly reveal-ing a reality that was previously unknown or unexperienced with-out the aid of the chemical catalyst; it is mind-expanding, not just mind-altering.[65] Each term is heavily weighted with philosophical assumptions.

Historically, the use of religious drugs for purposes of enlighten-ment has been associated with religions outside of those that hold there is one God—in particular, Christianity. The assumption behind the use of psychedelics is that through a transformation of con-sciousness one can—without divine mediation or revelation—directly intuit the mysteries of the cosmos. Christianity teaches that because humans are both finite and fallen they bear no such capacities—either on or off drugs. As Paul confessed, "For there is one God; there is also one mediator between God and humankind, Christ Jesus, himself human who gave himself a ransom for all."[66]

MAKING UP "REALITY"

The worldview of technoshamanism tends toward pantheistic monism, animism, and polytheism. Pantheistic monism is the plat-form for all occultism because it affirms that we are ultimately one with the one divine reality and have recourse to its powers through psychic techniques. Within this system, however, a variety of entities or energies are recognized as emanations or manifestations of the one reality. Hence a kind of operational animism or polytheism is the cousin of pantheistic monism, however illogical it may be to introduce a multiplicity of entities into an absolute unity. Tal Brooke, a writer on new religious movements, believes that cyberspace "by its very unitive structure, tends toward a kind of functional pantheism."[67] This seems to be the case for many who are already inclined toward the occult to various degrees, although the nature of cyberspace does not demand this kind of interpretation.

The responsible Christian should see cyberspace as a communications medium that shapes its contents in a bewildering variety of ways and thereby affects our selves and our culture. Our orientation toward the medium is crucial, as Paul highlighted long ago:

> To the pure all things are pure, but to those who are corrupted and do not believe, nothing is pure. In fact, both their minds and consciences are corrupted. They claim to know God, but by their actions they deny him.[68]

Leary and his cohorts have long despised monotheistic faiths that worship one God. In 1980 I heard Timothy Leary deliver a lecture (if one could so dignify it) in which he referred to the Judeo-Christian God as "the hanging judge God," who must be rejected because "reality is no larger than your mind." This kind of exuberant blasphemy is evident in the reincarnations of Leary's views in today's "cyberians." The cyberian worldview is shaped by the sensibilities of modern technologies, particularly those of cyberspace. As Rushkoff explains:

> According to cyberian logic, the grids of reality are creations. They are not necessarily real. . . . Anyone who has taken a psychedelic drug experiences this. Fantasy gamers play with this. Hackers who crack the "ice" of well-protected computer networks prove this. Anyone who has adopted the cyberian vision lives this.[69]

Rushkoff adds that cyberians rebel against dominant society not by crossing lines and breaking out of boxes, but by refusing to grant the reality of any lines or boxes. "The exploitation of these lines and boxes for fun is like playing hopscotch on the tablets of the Ten Commandments."[70] God as Lawgiver is off the screen.

Modern technopagans tend to be less romantic than their ancient ancestors concerning the ultimate mysteries of the cosmos.

They have, in good postmodernist fashion, abandoned the classical conception of truth and are simply playing with various contortions of consciousness. This assumption permeates Rushkoff's account of the cyberian worldview. Experiencing cyberspace and hallucinogens frees us from the tyranny of objective reality, meaning, and logic. Cyberians "have abandoned organized rules of logic in favor of reality hacking—riding the waves, watching for trends, keeping an open mind, and staying connected to the flow."[71] By "reality hacking," Rushkoff means viewing life as a game to played according to one's own rules: "Once all templates or characters become interchangeable, the gamer can 'infer' reality, because he has the ability to see it from any point of view he chooses."[72] The arbitrarily arranged rules of the computer game serve as a model of the universe at large. You make it up as you go along.

Reality hacking and the desire for a designer reality spun out of one's own head (via the proper hardware and software) rule out the notion of any fixed, final, and authoritative conception of reality. Reality moves from the objective singular to the subjective plural: there are many realities; hack the one you want. Yet in the same breath Rushkoff's cyberians and technopagans (the categories overlap, but are not identical) speak of reality as One (monism) and the divine as universally dispersed in everything (pantheism). They also sound animistic or polytheistic when they speak of particular spirits inhabiting cyberspace. Rushkoff even appeals to avant-garde theories in science for rational justification of his worldview. In so doing, he contradicts himself because he also says that there is "no such thing as non-fiction, only points of view."[73]

Reality-hacking without belief in a Reality that can be reached hollows out any claim of possessing a coherent worldview intellectually superior to any other worldview; it leaves only the rattling shells of arbitrary assertions. This high-tech relativism really boils down to a very noisy, cybercharged nihilism that employs mystical and magical terms to obscure its inner bankruptcy. This deception is what Francis Schaeffer called "semantic mysticism." Positive and engaging terms are used to cover up the emptiness of the worldview itself.[74] Jesus' indictment in a similar situation is apropos: "Woe to you, teachers of the law and Pharisees, you hypocrites! You are like whitewashed tombs, which look beautiful on the outside but on the inside are full of dead men's bones and everything unclean."[75]

Furthermore, in rejecting any absolute moral authority by opting for relativism, the technoshamanistic worldview unleashes an amoral anarchy impossible to restrain by the resources of its own thought. Technopagans may enjoy "playing hopscotch on the Ten Commandants," as Rushkoff says, but they will offer passionate protest when someone pirates their software or sends a hard disk–eating virus into their new computer system. Similarly, they morally object to the supposedly oppressive and dogmatic views of conservative Christians.

Such indignation has no foundation, given their worldview. It consists of mere assertions. Having abandoned logic as a test for truth, they are left with no reliable criteria for deciding which wave to surf or which trend to follow. How about hacking the neo-Nazi version of paganism (which is resurgent in Germany and elsewhere), or being open-minded about joining the ranks of the sexual predators who easily and happily move from virtual rape to the flesh-and-bone variety? Without recourse to a moral law above their own consciousness, without a transcendent standard for ethical evaluation, all moral protest or prescription must philosophically obliterate itself.

The domain of cyberspace does not in itself demand a descent into the high-tech deceptions of technoshamanism. But given the combined influence of the bewitching nature of cyberspace and the occult ideas thick in the cultural atmosphere, technoshamanism easily finds a digital domicile somewhere beyond the keyboards of its devotees. The soul, however, will not find its rest or wisdom there. Jaron Lanier, a pioneer in virtual reality technologies, sums it up: "The Internet exists for people to connect with each other. But to connect with the mystery of the universe, the Internet won't do. God doesn't have a Web site."[76]

As we have seen, whatever enticements it offers, technoshamanism suffers from an internally inconsistent and ultimately unlivable worldview. As Scripture affirms, "Unless the Lord builds the house, its builders labor in vain."[77] Jesus also taught that those who obey his teachings build their house on a rock that can withstand the vicissitudes of life, while those who fail to obey build only on shifting sand.[78] Erecting a worldview upon silicon is no better than building it on sand.

8

EXPLORING VIRTUAL COMMUNITY

CULTURE WATCHERS, SOCIAL CRITICS, politicians, clergy, theologians, philosophers, and just about everyone else within earshot have at least one thing in common today: They are all lamenting the loss of community and civility in American culture. Community consists of more than civility, but it must include civility, which philosopher Richard Mouw helpfully defines as "public politeness. It means that we display tact, moderation, refinement and good manners toward people who are different from us."[1] According to a recent cover story in *U.S. News & World Report*, Americans are not too successful at being civil. The article reported that 89 percent of Americans think incivility is a serious problem and that 78 percent believe it has worsened in the past ten years. Very large percentages of people agreed that incivility has contributed to violence (91 percent), a divided national community (85 percent), and eroding values (84 percent). Yet 99 percent say their own behavior is civil![2]

Columnist John Leo sees America as a "culture that celebrates impulse over restraint, notoriety over achievement, rule breaking over rule keeping and incendiary expression over minimal civility."[3] Leo believes the situation is critical: "Our levels of political, social and commercial discourse are now so low that it is surely time to try restoring civility from the bottom up. The alternative would seem to be an increasingly stupid and brutal culture."[4] The task is further complicated, however, by the absence of a common national identity and mission. We lack the ethos of a national community.

In his magisterial book *The American Hour*, Os Guinness eloquently articulates "the crisis of cultural authority" that grips, shakes, and drains our culture.[5] An increasingly pluralistic and self-centered America lacks a compelling social vision that would unify its voice, restrain its vices, define and reward its virtues, and direct its energies. As a result, we are engaged not in civil persuasion but in "culture wars" on a number of levels. Our national motto, *E pluribus unum* (out of many, one), is being called into question by multiculturalism, postmodernism, and the general cynicism of national life. The civic calling of America as "a city set on a hill" (the Puritans) or as "the almost chosen nation" (Abraham Lincoln) is sensed by few today. Americans remain somewhat patriotic, but in a self-serving sense of relishing their opportunities, freedom, and wealth; many have lost or are losing a larger national identity.

Instead of being a nation of citizens who are guided by transcendent ideals, we are becoming a nation of disputants who seek rights and entitlements without the corresponding responsibilities and duties. As Charles Sykes has rightly said, we are fast becoming "a nation of victims."[6] Adversaries make poor neighbors; our souls are not peace with one another. We are far from rejoicing with the psalmist: "How very good and pleasant it is when kindred live together in unity."[7]

COCOONING AGAINST COMMUNITY

The notion of community tends to erode under the conditions of postmodernity. A common social practice called "cocooning" isolates individuals from others by keeping them safe and snug in front of their home entertainment centers and computer screens when they could be playing with their children, talking to neighbors over the fence, or attending musical concerts, houses of worship, or block parties. Cocooning results from both the fear of rising violence in public places and the availability of entertainment in the home.[8] We may even take the cocoons with us by sonically insulating ourselves through our car stereo or Walkman.[9]

Futurist Edward Cornish observes that "the infomedia will tend to desocialize people, making them more prone to antisocial and criminal behavior." Before television and computers, "face-to-face conversation was the primary means of entertainment," which "trained people to deal with other people." But "the rise of electronic entertainment seems to have been accompanied by increasing rudeness, epitomized by drivers shooting each other in traffic accidents."[10] Cornish further worries that if electronic entertainment continues to infiltrate society,

> we may become a non-society—a poorly integrated mass of electronic hermits, unable to work well together because we no longer play together. Institutions such as the family, community, church, and nation will face the challenge of seeking support from people whose loyalty is almost entirely to themselves.[11]

Cocooning was taken to a rather bizarre extreme recently by Steve Mann, an MIT student who devised a mobile, head-mounted video display and camera that keeps him wired to cyberspace wherever he goes. The camera beams images to the Internet where people can see what he is seeing. The headgear also allows Mann to read e-mail, surf the Web, or work on his computer while going about his business. "I don't always have it on, but I've always got it with me," says Mann. He can choose to see the world through his eyes directly or through a video monitor in his visor that displays what the camera on his head is taking in. A story on "the man with three eyes" claims that "the effect of talking to Mann is disconcerting. His eyes shift between the person he is talking with and his computer screen."[12] Mann confesses, "There are times you want to be isolated. You still want to be aware of your surroundings but scale them down," he says as "his eyes are bathed in the cold white light of the tiny monitors in his visor."[13]

Mann's "human cam" is, for now, an experimental novelty, but it signals something on the horizon made possible by new cyberspace technologies: an eerie and precarious combination of presence and absence, of involvement and disengagement. A simulation of Mann's visual field is projected omnidirectionally through cyberspace, while he himself has difficulty being where he is. Mann's thesis advisor, Professor Rosalind Picard, believes that Mann's prototype is far from mass production, but that once the technical problems are ironed out the device might become as popular as the Walkman.[14] (In fairness, it should also be said that they hope the device might aid the visually impaired, a far more salutary goal.)

THE COMMUNITY WE CRAVE

Politics alone cannot enforce community, because community is pre-political in its essence; it is more a function of culture than of legislation. As Samuel Johnson said, "How small, of all that human hearts endure, / That part which laws or kings can cause or cure!" Communitarian writer Amitai Etzioni avers that some "measure of caring, sharing, and being our brother's and sister's keeper, is essential if we are not all to fall back on an ever more expansive government, bureaucratized welfare agencies, and swollen regulations, police, courts, and jails."[15]

The elements of local and national community, while not terribly hard to define, are terribly hard to achieve—at least in modern America. Nevertheless, as Richard John Neuhaus eloquently puts it, "We do indeed strive to build a world in which the strong are just and power is tempered by mercy, in which the weak are nurtured and the marginal embraced, and those at the entrance gates and those at the exit gates of life are protected both by law and love."[16]

Most of us would like to see a general civility where strangers can interact with patience, respect, and kindness; where families remain intact and mutually supportive of other families; where the downcast—whether physically or economically—are cared for largely by charitable organizations and individuals instead of being forgotten or pushed aside; where honesty, integrity, and humility become valued virtues; where arrogance, deceit, lewdness, and rudeness are rebuked and rejected; where shame and guilt police the conscience and provide spurs for moral growth; and where people consent to bear with their deepest differences—whether religious, political, or cultural—within constitutional constraints and without resorting to either spineless relativism or militant cultural combat—in short, where the golden rule is dusted off and put back on public display.

COMPUTERS, LOVE, AND COMMUNITY

When Polish political hero Lech Walesa first ventured out of the Soviet Bloc in 1988, he made this statement in Paris, "You have riches and freedom here but I feel no sense of faith or direction. You have so many computers, why don't you use them in the search for love?"[17] Is this possible or likely? Can computers aid us in the search for the love that binds communities together? Can e-mail, bulletin boards, data bases, and the rest really constitute a "virtual community" that makes for a real community? Is cyberspace the right kind of space for a meeting of souls?

Community was once reserved for persons closely associated geographically and culturally. Cyberspace technologies, however, have pushed the concept of community beyond these physical limits. Architect William Mitchell's insights are illuminating:

> As more and more business and social interaction shift into cyberspace, we are finding that accessibility depends even less on propinquity, and community has come increasingly unglued from geography. Our network connections are becoming as important as our bodily locations.[18]

Network connections may be as "important" in a cultural sense, but are they as significant, meaningful, and valuable? How readily should we jettison kinship and geography, proximity and contiguity? The living fibers of healthy community are many and complex, and we cannot touch on all of them here. But the notion that "community" can thrive in cyberspace challenges the very meaning of community and the nature of our sociality.

Paradoxically, although we live in McLuhan's "global village" through the aid of electronic media, our sense of village or community is languishing if not vanishing. David Wells incisively writes: "Our computers are starting to talk to us while our neighbors are becoming more distant and anonymous."[19] I may "connect" with terminals around the globe but know nothing of the pains, joys, and mundanities of the souls next door. As we remove ourselves from those who surround us physically, we attempt to compensate for our loneliness by connecting with those present only digitally.

Stephen Talbot wonders if "the widespread substitution of an abstract, 'information rich' discourse for a more muscular and human *present* interaction may be very much part of the formula for mutual alienation."[20] Being information-rich does not insure being relationship-rich. Talbot adds:

> A culture that has largely succeeded in eradicating the last traces of its own village life turns around and—by appealing to a yet fur-

ther extension of the eradicating technology—encourages itself with Edenic images of a global village. This is Doublespeak.[21]

Quite so. Doublespeak presents a self-contradictory message: the very technologies—radio, television, computer—that have tended to isolate us from personal contact with others will bring us into a global village of intimate connection. When almost everything is mediated by technology and so much of our "interaction" is electronic and not natural, there is no reason to expect that the bonds of sociability will grow and strengthen. As Gregory Stock puts it: "No wonder the emotional links between humans and the 'natural' environment are weakening; an ever growing fraction of human experience is in an entirely different realm."[22]

ON THE INTERNET, NOBODY KNOWS YOU'RE A DOG

A now famous cartoon in the *New Yorker* shows one dog saying to another, "On the Internet, nobody knows you're a dog." We have touched on the problem of truth in cyberspace as well as its disembodied character, but the element of the equality of its participants needs to be considered. In *The Road Ahead*, his best-selling cheer for everything digital, Bill Gates states a commonly heard refrain about the beneficial aspects of cyberspace communication. Exulting in the fact that "anyone can send anyone else a message on the Internet," Gates comments that correspondents "who might be uncomfortable talking to each other in person have forged bonds across a network." Gates laments, though, that the much-heralded information highway will "do away with the social, racial, gender, and species blindness that text-only exchanges permit" because of its incorporation of video.[23]

Gates's comment is curious. First, it is not true that "anyone can send anyone else a message on the Internet." This is true for Gates and his friends, to be sure; but most people are still strangers to cyberspace either because they lack the stamina to master a new and often intimidating technology or because they simply do not have the financial resources to connect. Today's users of the Internet are overwhelmingly young, white, middle to upper-middle class, and male—although the rate of women involved (31.5 percent) seems to be increasing fairly rapidly.[24]

Connections of various kinds are being made through cyberspace, but, as yet, these electronic rendezvous do not seem to be crossing gender, class, and racial barriers in any significant way. In fact, many worry that the juggernaut of advancing cyberspace technologies will leave many minorities and disadvantaged people out of the loop. For instance, a 1989 study by the U.S. Census Bureau found that although computer use and ownership was increasing rapidly, only 1.5 million African Americans used computers at home, compared to 26.9 million whites. Of course, computer use and ownership is positively correlated with higher income levels.[25] This may change somewhat, though, if the cost of computers continues to plummet while their capacities increase.

Even if computers become more affordable for more people, how will poorer folks learn how to use them, especially if schools in lower-income neighborhoods have less access to computer education?[26] As Clifford Stoll has pointed out, the cyberspace community is not as friendly as it often presents itself to be. Because of the "exclusionary nature of technocratic culture," it is up to the user to figure out what system is best, to decipher the new, jargon-heavy terminology, and to install and maintain the software.[27] The result is that outsiders are often put off by "a liturgy of technology."[28]

Second, the anonymity of nonvideo interaction in cyberspace is not what Gates and others claim it to be. There is reason to be skeptical abut the idea that the disembodied and largely anonymous character of cyberspace will "teach us to value quickness of mind over beauty, wit over physical power, the content of our characters over the color of our skin."[29] On the one hand, textual communication can be a leveler. On the screen, one is only as good or bad as his or her words. I can imagine people conversing through e-mail who might otherwise avoid each other. If the more impersonal medium enhances the personal dimension instead of eclipsing it, these online relationships could be converted into more full-blooded off-screen encounters.

On the other hand, I am afraid this pleasant scenario requires a basic honesty and integrity that the culture of cyberspace often lacks. Assuming a false identity in order to deceive someone is lying, pure and simple. What kind of civil relationship can be founded on deception? Furthermore, the particularities of race, age, gender, and economic status cannot be forever erased if people are to know each other as embodied beings in the physical world. A racist may converse online with someone of another race, whom he comes to appreciate as being a good writer, well educated, and friendly. The crunch comes, though, when the racist finds that his e-mail correspondent is typing with differently pigmented hands. If the racial anonymity is never broken, no progress toward racial reconciliation can be forged. If racial realities are revealed and prejudice continues, nothing has been changed. The same problems occur for age, gender, and economic status. What kind of community is being created when the members are digitally sheared of these characteristics? Clay Shirky wisely observes, "An area that bases its idea of tolerance on simply hiding the characteristics the majority are intolerant of is at best a digital closet."[30]

Community worthy of its name is largely fashioned out of the recognition of our embodied and sometimes awkward particularities, within a context of regarding one another as fellow humans worthy of respect and civility. The Christian deepens this by adding that people are made in the image and likeness of God; they are not only our neighbors, they are objects of divine concern. Writing in 1966, management expert Peter Drucker wisely saw that "throughout the ages the problem has always been how to get 'communication' out of information."[31]

> Now suddenly we are in a situation in which information is largely impersonal and, therefore, without any communications content. It is pure information. But now we have the problem of establishing the necessary minimum of communications so that we understand each other and can know each other's needs, goals, perceptions, and ways of doing things. Information does not supply this. Only direct contact, whether by voice or by written word, can communicate.[32]

When Drucker wrote of the "direct contact" of the "written word," he knew nothing of such technologies as e-mail and chat rooms. He was thinking of personal notes, memos, and letters, which are more directly personal and not as subject to the identity confusions and deceptions of cyberspace. Information exchanged in cyberspace can easily mask or ignore one's "needs, goals, perceptions, and ways of doing things." Civil communities—places where a soul may flourish with other souls—ask us to present ourselves as we really are before others as they really are, that we might learn where we agree, where we disagree, how to disagree agreeably, and how to persuade each other through compassion and reason.

Cyberspace Sensibilities and Community

Disagreeing agreeably is particularly taxing in cyberspace. I briefly mentioned the problem of "flaming" earlier. A flame is an uncivil information bomb launched from one computer toward another. The disembodied context of cyberspace is highly conducive to such textual attacks. As Martin Hash, a developer of animation software, observes, "People with an otherwise dull, mundane, unexceptional life could become whoever they want to be in the anonymity of Net culture. It is amazing how the brittle mantle of civility is shattered if even the thinnest veil of anonymity is provided."[33] Given the nature of this medium, incivility could become habitual and spill over into the offline world. Again, as McLuhan said, "We become what we behold."[34] More importantly, the apostle Paul warned, "Bad company corrupts good character."[35]

Craig Brod and other psychologists have found in case studies that those who are compulsively involved with computers "are much more intolerant of behavior that is at all ambiguous, digressive, or tangential." Of course, such behavior is a large part of being a human, rather than a computer program. "In their interaction with spouses, family, and acquaintances, they are often terse, preferring simple yes-no [binary] responses."[36] Brod notes that these people prefer to "transfer information quickly. People who talk too slowly or in general terms are avoided or ignored."[37] They just cannot process information quickly enough. So much for civil communication. In an insightful *New Yorker* article called "My First Flame," John Seabrook speaks of a computer whiz who had "that intense energy you often see in guys who are really into computers; the speed at which he talks and moves always makes me think of the clatter of fingers over the keyboard."[38] Of course, Seabrook's friend may have always been frenetic; the computer, however, lends itself to that sensibility.

The velocity at which information travels is both a gift and a curse. When my friends in France sent me an emergency prayer request by e-mail, it reached me much faster than it would have by regular mail. This allowed me to pray immediately, since time was of the essence. The increased speed of information exchange, however, can induce impatience with anything that happens more slowly. While information may fly across the globe at nearly the speed of light, direct contact with human beings continues to form the deeper civilities required for community. Social critic Jeremy Rifken points out that "in every culture up to now the temporal order has been established primarily around face-to-face interaction, with other forms of communications existing as extensions of that interaction." Now, however, computer technology threatens to set the pace and define the terms of communication by its mechanical structures.[39]

Nicholas Negroponte laments that the speed and low cost at which e-mail can be transmitted may mean that "a single carriage return can dispatch fifteen or fifty thousand unwelcome words into your [electronic] mailbox. That simple act turns e-mail from a personal and conversational medium into wholesale dumping."[40] Information dumping is not the stuff of civil conversation, to be sure. I myself was guilty of Negroponte's complaint when I sent him a file of an article I wrote on technology shortly after (I thought) I had learned to work such marvels. He e-mailed back a sentence fragment along the lines of "came out as garbage."

As we have seen in this chapter, virtual community may be too virtual to serve as the kind of community we crave. Prejudice and bigotry need stronger antidotes than the anonymity of cyberspace. Communication may actually be diminished in the velocities of digital space. And as we will see in the next chapter, other aspects of community may also have a hard time surviving, let alone thriving, in cyberspace.

9

VIRTUAL COMMUNITY: TRUST, DECEPTION, AND INFECTION

COMMUNITY IS IMPOSSIBLE without some level of trust, even among strangers. We try to live in a good neighborhood where we can trust those around us not to accost us or harm our property. We must trust our accountants and our medical doctors to be reasonably competent with our assets and our bodies. How much can cyberspace reinforce trust? Social scientist Francis Fukuyama puts a damper on some cyberoptimists, such as Al Gore, the Tofflers, George Gilder, and Newt Gingrich, who think that computer technologies will decentralize knowledge, eliminate hierarchies of all sorts, and liberate the masses from political oppression. He writes that "trust does not reside in integrated circuits or fiber optic cables. Although it involves an exchange of information, trust is not reducible to information."[1] Rather, "trust is the expectation that arises within a community of regular, honest, and cooperative behavior, based on [the] commonly shared norms . . . of other members of that community."[2]

DECEPTION IN CYBERSPACE

Steward Brand, a cyberguru and founder of the WELL online service in San Francisco, reports that in 1982 a group of forty people established a private online network associated with a research institute in La Jolla. After six months of cyberbliss, an unidentified member began to post flames. Soon the group became so obsessed with uncovering the flamer that all profitable discussion died. The uncivil cybernaut was never found out. Brand explains that "not only did this break up the online community—it permanently affected the *trust* that those people had for each other in the face-to-face world, because they were never able to figure out who did it. To this day, they don't know which one of them it was."[3]

In many ways, the nature of cyberspace is conducive to deception, as we have mentioned earlier concerning gender surfing and the adoption of assumed identities. Deceptions on the Internet can reach far beyond a few fake identities in MUDs and MOOs, however. On April 20, 1995, the day after the Oklahoma City bombing, a message was posted in the Usenet database (misc.activism.militia) that read:

> OK City bombed by FBI. Now they begin their black campaign in order to spread as much terror as possible. . . . They will try to tie it to Waco. Janet Reno is behind this, the campaign will succeed because the media will persuade the public. Expect a crackdown. Bury your guns and use the codes.[4]

This message was mentioned in the *San Francisco Chronicle*, *USA Today*, *Newsday*, the *Atlanta Journal-Constitution*, and other newspapers, all alarmed at the frightening prospects it evoked. The creator of the message, however, was not a wild-eyed extremist but a journalism student at the University of Montana who posted the message as a joke.[5] The article in *Internet Underground* that reported on this prank also lists an "Internet Hoax Hall of Fame," which includes claims about alien autopsies, Microsoft buying the Vatican, the modem tax, and fake political web pages.[6]

Why are these deceptions so common and so difficult to detect? The author of the *Internet Underground* article, Bob King, insightfully notes that:

> The 'net is a communications medium with no deterrent against falsehood. Nobody can see or hear you, or tell for sure where you are, or judge the truth of half the things you say. In a world where people are just floating characters on a screen, you can afford to burn a few bridges.[7]

He further comments that while some have learned to be skeptical of other media, they tend to be more gullible before the computer screen, "as though the 'net were a gateway to secret knowledge about political conspiracies and investment tips."[8] A popular cyberspace slogan says that "information wants to be free"; but free information may not be true.[9]

The use of video combined with the Internet (one of the promises of the information highway) does not assure verity either, since video morphing technologies make simulations appear incredibly real. Martin Hash, an expert on computer simulation, predicts that within a decade, "cyberspace will be occupied with CG [cartoon graphics] characters that are indistinguishable from real people."[10] The old adage "seeing is believing" is now itself unbelievable, at least with respect to electronic media. The digital darkening of O. J. Simpson's face on the cover of *Time* magazine is a case in point. No one would have known the difference had not *Newsweek* ran the same mug shot without the alteration. This type of digital deception can be perpetrated in cyberspace as well, and may never be exposed.[11]

An alarming article in the *Scientific American* by William J. Mitchell states that "we are approaching the point at which most of the images that we see in our daily lives, and that form our understanding of the world, will have been digitally recorded, transmitted and processed."[12] Altered photos were far more easily discerned before digital manipulations became available. Today, "digital images are manipulated by altering pixel values stored in computer memory rather than by mechanically altering surfaces."[13] This process hides the alterations quite nicely. Mitchell predicts that "the information superhighway will bring us a growing flood of visual information in digital format, but we will have to take great care to sift the facts from the fictions and the falsehoods."[14] The necessity of such constant suspicion hardly builds trusting communities.

Cinematic wizard George Lucas has recently been cutting back on payroll by using computer simulations for crowd scenes. In the movie *The American President*, Michael Douglas is shown giving the State of the Union address. But he is not in the House of Representatives, nor are there really fifteen hundred people in attendance. The congressional setting was digitally added and an actual "crowd" of eighty was multiplied to fifteen hundred through digital replication and enhancement.[15]

Entire mass events can now be simulated and broadcast either on television or through cyberspace. Actors can be created out of nothing by computer as well. The movie *Casper*, about a ghost, starred a completely digital image. A 1996 article in *Forbes* predicts that there will be a movie starring a fake human by the end of the decade.[16]

More and more aspects of films are being shot on location—in cyberspace, that is—with the likes of the dinosaurs of *Jurassic Park* or the entire cast of *Toy Story*.[17] A recently produced beer commercial features the deceased John Wayne as the main character. Hyperrealities are being multiplied and magnified everywhere, often without a clue that they are in fact hyperrealities and not ordinary realities. The very idea of an object becomes uncertain in this vicinity.

BOTS IN CYBERSPACE

The matter of trust and deception is further complicated by the presence of robots (or "bots") mimicking humans in cyberspace. One of the wonders of cyberspace is the personalized impersonality of it. One night I received an e-mail message from the *New York Times* explaining how I could use their online service. After reading the clearly written message, I noticed that the "author" was The New York Times Subscriber Robot. In this case, the impersonation by the impersonal was transparent, but this is not always so.

Bots lurk in cyberspace. A bot is short for robot, but not the kind that moves objects or scurries about taking factory jobs away from people in real life. A bot is a computer program that impersonates a person in cyberspace. They are common in MUDs and may appear elsewhere as well.

"Julia" is a bot designed for MUDs by Artificial Intelligence expert Michael Maudlin at Carnegie Mellon University. She began to stalk cyberspace in 1991. Sherry Turkle notes that, "among other things, in the context of a MUD, Julia is able to chat about hockey, keep track of players' whereabouts, and flirt."[18] Julia also possesses some traits that most humans lack, given her superior "memory." Since Julia operates in regions thick with predatory males, she often repels advances with an acerbic and rather raw wit.[19] Julia, also known as "chatterbot," has fooled many people into thinking she was human—although the silicon was let out of the bag in 1993 and some fed-up non-bots held an unsuccessful "Kill Julia" contest.[20]

Another more political bot is "Sedar Argic," a.k.a. "Zumabot," who began cruising the Internet in 1988 and posting diatribes about Turkish culture in a number of newsgroups related to Turkey or politics. Sedar would look for key words and phrases in postings and then flame the sender. The response would include a relevant section of the original posting peppered with insults and a tirade about supposed massacres of Muslims in Armenia during World War I. It would be sent to the original newsgroup and often cross-posted to other groups, "to ensure maximum victim humiliation."[21] The Zumabot's flames sometimes consumed the innocent, however. Being programmed to post in groups with the word "Turkey" in them, he went batty around Thanksgiving, attacking anyone who mentioned the main dish. *Internet Underground* believes that Sedar "may have worked for a foreign intelligence agency for propaganda purposes."[22]

Less sophisticated programs than Julia and Sedar Argic have deceived the electronic elect. A program called ELIZA mimics conversation without benefit of actual artificial intelligence. Nevertheless, ELIZA convinced one cybernaut to confess to her some intimate secrets of his sex life! Other bots called "agent programs" are being used to answer questions, do automatic mailings, and administer ongoing e-mail discussions.[23]

Although we may occasionally be tricked by a cross-dresser or impersonator in real life, it would be unusual to mistake a machine for a person. The range of artifice is somewhat limited by the contours of bodily presence. Few such restrictions exist in cyberspace. One may be having a dialog that is really a monologue. A call-out quotation in the *Internet Underground* article cited above is quite telling: "Sure, they may just be circuitry, but computers can be better conversationalists than the people you meet online."[24] This kind of mentality, even if hyperbole, can only cheapen our respect for other persons in community. Instead of learning sexual propriety offline, for example, one might prefer sex-talk online with "Julia."

Bots may also be writing what appears to be written by human authors. One software package helps write evaluations for employees by using stock content. Instead of esteeming the personal touch in the difficult area of performance reviews, some are opting for programs to do much of the work for them. The golden rule should be applied here. Would the supervisors who use such a program want *their* superiors to give them a report that was really written by a bot?

Bots are also intruding on journalism. Futurist Edward Cornish reports that a Nebraska newspaper is employing a "software program that can write sports stories; once the computer gets a few facts, it can fill in the rest of the words to make a breathless report of a game."[25] It literally is a breathless report, since no human is breathing on the other side of the print. Would these "stories" carry the byline of a human? If so, deception is added to impersonality.

Given that the respective identities of humans and machines can be so easily confused in cyberspace, one wonders just what kind of community this might be. Simulated personality may be fascinating, but how can interaction with a bot help civilize us, help us work through challenges and difficulties with real people? Moreover, if the nature of much of cyberspace communication is such that it can be duplicated by a bot, how deeply personal and truly communicative can it be—even when it is between humans?[26]

THE "PERSONAL" AGENT

Cyberspace enthusiasts, such as Bill Gates and Nicholas Negroponte, hype the powers of the "personal agent," a bot that serves as a gatekeeper of the information available from the Internet. Given the current information overload, such a function is deemed necessary to separate the desirable from the undesirable. Such agents already exist, but Gates waxes ecstatic over the prospect of agents being used in the anticipated information highway.

> Perhaps the most intriguing approach [to navigating the digital data], and the one that promises to be the easiest of all to use, will be to enlist the aid of a *personal agent* who will represent you on the highway. The agent will actually be software, but it will have a *personality* you'll be able to talk to in one form or another. This will be like delegating an assistant to look at the inventory for you.[27]

Without batting an eyelash (or dimming a screen), Gates depersonalizes our interaction with information and personalizes inanimate machinery. The agent is "personal" in that we program it, but it is not a person with insight, imagination, or conscience. Gates's scenario is not like "delegating an assistant to look at the inventory for you," because an assistant is a person with a soul who can exercise good judgment, kindness, and wisdom, or poor judgment, cruelty, and stupidity. In the desire to harness information with maximum efficiency ("the *easiest* of all to use"), Gates dispenses with all human interaction with information. In his digitopia, machines do the sorting for us.

So much for the librarian's years of research skills that can be deftly applied to my particular needs. So much for consulting with scholars whose judgment I respect. So much for bumping into a lay philosopher in the library while browsing the stacks. When we give over our involvement with information to the discretion of impersonal agents, we lose our association with the community of human knowledge. We could gain a world of predigested information at the cost of our souls.

Cybrarian Reva Basch believes "the most salable commodity in cyberspace is going to be point of view," whereby you assign a "knowbot" to search out information that fits your desires. You could command: " 'OK, Rush Limbaugh knowbot,' or 'OK, Ralph Nader knowbot, go out there and get me stuff from the Net that you think is important.' "[28] The problem of stridently ideological thinking—holding a position firmly without engaging in intellectual discourse to justify it—could be easily multiplied when the personal agent provides information from only one point of view. Of course, one might use both the Rush and Ralph knowbots to compare notes, but how much would be lost in the middle?

However sophisticated the agent, computer programs cannot determine truth or meaning, as was evidenced by the bot that mistook turkey the bird for Turkey the country. Agents and other search engines may be digitally "powerful" (a word used with total abandon by digitopians when fawning over their new technologies), but clueless on simple matters of research beyond its programming. James Fallows explains that although computer searches are "extremely fast and accurate," one must know exactly what to look for.

> If the article you were thinking of appeared one day before or after your target period, or if the names you were looking for were twenty-one rather than twenty words part, or if owing to a newspaper typo 'Clinton' became 'Clnton,' you would not find those articles, and you would never know how close you came.[29]

Fallows still appreciates these search systems, but his comments reveal their limitations. Stoll notes that computer-generated indexes to books have awesome power but no intellect. For instance, "Jumbo the Pachyderm won't get indexed under 'elephant.' "[30]

Gates's love affair with the digital has dimmed his vision of the uniquely human horizon. This is evident throughout his book, as when he glories in "friction-free capitalism" that will eliminate more and more human agents from the economic marketplace—in order to lessen costs and increase productivity, of course![31] Gary Chapman concludes a revealing article called "Friction-Free Economy? No Jobs. Aye, There's the Rub," by saying,

> Beneath the celebratory rhetoric about the coming 'friction-free' economy is a ticking time bomb: the explosive idea that tens of millions of workers can be summed up, and shunted aside, as mere friction.[32]

People are notorious for their friction-production; silicon, on the other hand, is frictionless (and unalive). The cyberspace of Gates's expectations is not a place where I want to live. I probably would be unemployed anyway, put out on the streets by a philosopher/professor know-it-all bot.

Negroponte claims that what "we today call 'agent-based interfaces' will emerge as the dominant means by which computers and people talk with one another."[33] Personal agents are already available to select your entertainment, whether music, movies, books, or television shows. Why bother to consult friends, talk with people in stores (who are already more absorbed by computer read-outs than the actual inventory), or browse through the hard stuff for yourself? Personal entertainment–selection agents can do it all, further eroding the personal contact required for a community of souls.[34] This takes cocooning to new depths. Not only do we consume our entertainment alone, we select it without any human assistance.

Soon everything will be mediated by machines. Being digital will replace being there, being personal. In the acknowledgments to his best-selling book *Being Digital,* Negroponte thanks a woman who "runs my office and runs me." He adds, "Really intelligent computer agents are far off in time, so having an excellent human one is important (and rare)."[35] I wonder if this woman realized that she was being thanked for doing a job that Negroponte believes a machine would

one day do for him. Negroponte's compliment entailed the expectation of her eventual unemployment.

The replacement of the direct experience of humans in natural
community by machines fits a disturbing larger social pattern, identified by Jean Baudrillard:

> A kind of generalized derogation is occurring, whereby wish, abil-
> ity and knowledge, though not forsaken, are being surrendered to
> another, a second *agency*. Already, in any case, the filter of screen,
> photographs, video images and news reporting allows us access
> only to that which has already been seen by others. We are indeed
> incapable of apprehending anything that has not already been
> seen. We have assigned machines the task of seeing for us—just
> as, before long, we shall assign computers the task of making all
> our decisions.[36]

VIRTUAL INFECTION

With the augmented efficiency of cyberspace connections in a *virtual* community comes the threat of a *viral* community. The greater
the connectivity, the greater the potential for infection. The greater
the velocity of data transfer, the greater the ferocity of data corruption. When people began exploring and colonizing the new world,
they brought with them new diseases for which indigenous peoples
had no immunity. Countless people died. Similarly, the exploration
and colonization of cyberspace have created a "global village" of electronic information transfer.[37] Enter the computer virus—for which
the electronic "village" seems to have no immunity.

Until recently, viruses were only biological. Now they are also
digital, wreaking havoc in computers connected by cable across thousands of miles. These infectious programs can erase hard disks, corrupt data, and inflict all manner of ill, according to the perverse
proficiencies of the hackers who create the viruses. A number of
rumored but unreal viruses have caused almost as much stress as the
real thing. The global village could even experience a global plague if
we were all to get wired to the wrong program. Robert Seabrook
describes the terror he experienced when he feared a worm (a kind
of virus) had been planted in his computer through e-mail: "In my
excitement over the new medium, I had not considered that in going

online I was placing my work and my most private musing only inches from a roaring highway of data . . . [that] didn't care about me."[38]

There are more frightened travelers and road-kill than one might think. Twice while I was in a supposedly Christian chat room, a vicious character hurled blasphemous and infantile insults at everyone and then typed in strange symbols that caused my computer to give an error message and cease to function. The problem disappeared after shutting down the computer and restarting it (assuming he has not planted a digital time bomb), but it was quite an unexpected attack from cyberspace. I did not even know I was at risk. I have since learned that entire books and journals are dedicated to exploring new ways of writing and delivering computer viruses.[39]

Hackers have successfully cracked the Pentagon's computer system, stolen millions of digitally recorded dollars, carried out unauthorized surveillance, and much more. With any new mass-implemented technology comes new powers for evil. Think twice before using your credit card in cyberspace or divulging any secret there. Electronic privacy is impossible to insure. It is all recorded somewhere and someone has access to it, whether this access is legal or not.

Computer expert Winn Schwartau warns that "the essence of our very being is distributed across thousands of computers and data bases over which we have little or no control."[40] I would not call information communicated over the Internet "the essence of our very being," but Schwartau has a point. Moreover, "the sad fact is that these records which define us as an individual remain unprotected, subject to malicious modification, unauthorized disclosure, or out-and-out destruction."[41] Schwartau's in-depth book *Information Warfare* is a startling expose of these kinds of problems. The global village is potentially a very frightening place; there may be no place to hide your data.

Besides technologically conceived viruses, cyberspace is an amenable medium for what Douglas Rushkoff calls "media viruses," which refer to the ways ideas infect the masses at rapid speeds and in novel ways through electronic media.[42] The delivery system of the Internet makes possible the dissemination of ideas that bypasses the traditional intermediaries of editorial control, paper publishing, material transport, and so on. Of course, this can be used for good or ill;

but particularly virulent ideas can pollute people's minds in unprecedented ways through cyberspace.

Emerge, which calls itself "Black America's newsmagazine," recently ran an expose of racist groups who are exploiting the Internet with evangelistic determination. Various white supremacist cadres—neo-Nazis, Skinheads, identity groups, and others—are employing sophisticated technologies to proselytize. In April of 1996, a Skinhead group disseminated a photograph of a prone black man being kicked by a white person.[43] Another hate-mongering group advocates taking advantage of cyberspace anonymity to post injurious messages that appear to be written by "the enemy" (African Americans). They also advise other despicable racist practices.[44] One white supremacist declares that "cyberguerrillas" should "grasp the weapon which is the Net, and wield it skillfully."[45]

Of course, such irrational prejudice has been alive since sin entered the world, but cyberspace opens new doors for the kind of racial acrimony that acts like an acid upon our efforts to establish a multiracial community. A number of civil rights groups, such as the Klanwatch Project of the Southern Poverty Law Center, are attempting to monitor such groups. Angie Lowry of the Klanwatch Project observes: "Their Web pages are amazingly sophisticated. They are very readable and have good graphs. The Net makes it easier for those who share their views to reach them than in the old days, when you had to send $20 to a post office box and wait for a brochure."[46] The Internet also allows such clandestine groups to network with each other as never before. Unless decent people make a concerted and courageous stand for racial equality and reconciliation, the burning cross may shoot out sparks that spread like wildfire in the corrupted sectors of cyberspace.

ALZHEIMER'S ONLINE

Despite the many hazards to community that cyberspace presents, the medium can help create and solidify community when it is used carefully and is tethered to the real world in tangible ways. Although *Wired* magazine is usually consumed with the young and restless world of cutting-edge (and off-the-edge) cyberspace technologies and philosophies, recently it devoted a thoughtful piece to a project that helps spouses of Alzheimer's sufferers find a sense of community online.

The Alzheimer's online project installed computers in the homes of Alzheimer's victims for the purpose of connecting spouses who feel isolated, overwhelmed, and hopeless. A special network was developed and the procedures for sending e-mail were simplified and explained, since those over sixty-five typically have little experience with computers. At the time of the article's writing over two hundred people had participated, including a man named Linus who says that the computer "became my life-line. If someone came up to me and said they were going to take it back, I'd say 'Take my left arm instead.' "[47]

For these needy folks, cyberspace has become a place to give and receive advice and encouragement; it is a medium that met a desperate need when nothing else was available. Alzheimer's patients absorb tremendous amounts of time and energy at any hour of the day or night. This is especially taxing on aged spouses, who have little opportunity for normal socializing or recreation. Given these severe physical limitations, the ease and rapidity of e-mail has provided solace for these isolated souls. Often the electronic contact has been followed up by phone calls and face-to-face meetings.

In 1995, the National Information Infrastructure Awards selected the online Alzheimer's project out of 150 applications for its first annual Community Award. Scott Bascon, a spokesperson for the group, rightly said that the project "exemplifies what it means to live in a networked society. Here we have lives enriched. Here, technology is used to break down some very difficult barriers."[48]

What made the online Alzheimer's project work as a support group? Although it has been successful in alleviating suffering and bringing knowledge and friendship to those otherwise isolated, the project does not dignify all things digital. In this case, the people involved took up the technology as a last resort: other avenues toward community had been shut off because of the extremity of their situation. (This, however, may not always be true for those who care for spouses afflicted with Alzheimer's.) In addition, the senior citizens were carefully assisted by computer-savvy people who helped them set up the e-mail networks free of charge.

Few people ever experience this kind of personalized initiation into cyberspace. Furthermore, the sensibilities of the participants in this project had been formed in a precomputer age. They tended, it seemed, to view the medium as a variation of letter-writing that allowed for greater speed and more connections with other people. Many of the relationships that developed through e-mail were translated into more personal interactions at a later time. Nevertheless, the ways in which this online support group helped sustain a community of similarly suffering people could serve as a model for the wise use of cyberspace.

Generally speaking, the kind of community required for the resuscitation of national life requires the grace that comes through the human touch, the human voice, the human gaze. Genuine community shines through the human presence of truth expressed personally. Cyberspace can only mimic or mirror these things (however convincingly); it cannot create them. It can, however, beguile us into mistaking connectivity for community, data for wisdom, and efficiency for excellence. If cyberspace is kept closely fastened to the real world, and if we refuse its temptations to exchange the virtual for the literal, it can be our servant. Otherwise it will become a demanding and all-consuming media master.

10

ONLINE CHRISTIANITY?

Today many of the cyberspace technologies are being readily appropriated in Christian circles. For instance, a number of software programs claim to expedite or even revolutionize our knowledge of the Bible. Some interactive CD-ROMs contain the entire text of the Scriptures (sometimes in the original languages), study tools, and even video clips. Hypertext links enable the user to move about from one feature to another almost instantly. The entire Bible is now at our fingertips. If, for example, I want to find every instance of the word *world* in the New International Version, King James Version, and Living Bible, I punch a few keys and the information is before me. There is no need to haul out a bulky concordance.

Some radio hosts bring their Bible software with them into the studio to help callers deal with Bible questions. They boot up their laptops, run their programs, and furtively hit keys in search of Scripture verses. As a frequent radio-show guest, I have observed several hosts and guests work their machines. Interestingly, I have always been able to beat them to the Scriptures either through memory (that ancient, low-tech method) or by paging through my well-worn *NIV Study Bible*. In some cases, their expensive and "powerful" programs have emitted strange, unsolicited sounds and resolutely refused to produce the desired texts. Their computers' promise of speedy access and ready reference failed to deliver while my old and well-worn friend, "the Good *Book*," did its job nicely. Why was this?

The answer goes beyond computer incompetence. The radio hosts I described are solid Christians who know the Bible—probably better than I do. They brought their laptops to help others, not to compensate for their ignorance. My advantage was that I brought my own Bible, with my highlighting, notes, and bookmarks. There is something irreplaceable about that kind of physical history that no computer program can match, however powerful.

JIGSAWING SCRIPTURE

Hypertext capacities in Bible software present another potential snare. Users may end up dissecting the Bible into info-chunks instead of understanding the Scripture's context, historical setting, and overall theological significance. I may call up seventeen references to repentance, string them together, and print them out for sermon material—without understanding the nuances of each reference in its original literary context, whether narrative, wisdom, poetic, or didactic. Information retrieval is not synonymous with handling the truth wisely.[1] Since computers cannot discern meaning, we cannot expect them to deliver wisdom. That is up to us, with God's help.

As historian Mark Noll remarks in *The Scandal of the Evangelical Mind*, American fundamentalists and evangelicals tended to chop up the Bible into information bits even before the advent of cyberspace technologies. Instead of viewing the Scriptures as a unified whole of various kinds of literature, all of which reveal God's truth, conservative Protestants often construct a cut-and-paste theology by lifting passages out of their settings and arranging them into topical categories.

Noll notes that these trends from the nineteenth century still "undercut the possibility for a responsible intellectual life" among many evangelicals. There remains "a weakness for treating the verses of the Bible as pieces in a jigsaw puzzle that [need] only to be sorted and then fit together to possess a finished picture of divine truth."[2] The task of systematic theology requires that we understand and order the propositional claims of the entire Scripture. The cut-and-paste method ignores the need to understand the Bible as a whole, instead focusing on superficial interpretations of isolated texts. Hypertext biblical software may well accentuate this unfortunate tendency and further remove us from the Bible's own meaning.

Worse yet would be the use of programs that structure sermons or Bible lessons for us, in the same way that some programs write personnel evaluations and sports stories with minimal human involvement (see chapter nine). This would be a form of digital plagiarism.[3] Pastors are disciplined or even dismissed for preaching other people's sermons, and rightly so. The pastor who resorts to a computer sermon is preaching a sermon that has been written, in part, by a computer program. Instead of laboring over the text, trembling before the Word of God, and earnestly praying for wisdom to speak the truth in love with power to the church, the pastor opts for a generic message that is uninspired and inauthentic.

With an array of Bible facts before us, all neatly categorized by our software, we may be mesmerized into thinking that we have mastered the Scriptures when we have mastered only the software (or at least part of it). Derrick de Kerckhove, Director of the University of Toronto's McLuhan Program, seizes this point concerning the availability of information:

> Why bother learning all this stuff yourself if you have access to it when you need it? Quite the reverse, you might find value in not knowing something, as the very process of discovering anything may be more useful and exciting than the content of the discovery. With real expert [computer] systems, improved by sophisticated neural networks with rapid learning curves, you don't need to be an expert in anything.[4]

SUBSTITUTING COMPUTERS FOR INTELLECT

Pascal wrote that human "memory is necessary for all the operations of reason,"[5] yet the tendency today is for people to rely more on their computer's memory than on their own. Could it become more exciting to use lightning-fast search functions to call up biblical texts and tools than to "hide the word in our heart" and meditate upon it before God?[6] This is a constant temptation in the culture of cyberspace. The answer to the epidemic of biblical illiteracy and theological ignorance is not the availability of more information. Rather the answer comes in the shaping of our sensibilities such that an understanding of biblical truth becomes consequential and foundational in our lives.

Throwing Bible software at souls who have not learned to dwell richly on the Word of God as objectively, absolutely, and universally true will hardly be of help. Pollster George Barna asked "born again

Christians" if they agreed with the following statement: "There is no such thing as absolute truth; two people could define truth in totally conflicting ways, but both could still be correct." In 1991, 52 percent agreed with this statement. By 1994 it had shot up to 62 percent, a rate of increase faster than in the secular world.[7] The problem of truth decay runs far deeper than what technology can cure. This mass defection from Christ as the one and final truth requires nothing less than repentance and reeducation at the deepest possible levels.[8]

Although the intended purpose and content of Bible software may be wonderful, the effects of these technologies may end up contradicting what was intended. Instead of becoming more like the lauded Bereans, who received Paul's "message with great eagerness and examined the Scriptures every day to see if what Paul said was true,"[9] we might become more like the church at Laodicea who thought itself rich and in need of nothing when in reality it was spiritually "poor, blind, and naked" and in need of repentance.[10]

In contrast, if one's sensibilities have been formed through sustained interaction with the Bible as a book, the use of Bible programs can be supportive. For instance, a friend of mine has frequently been a guest on a national radio call-in program. He tells me that he brings his laptop computer into the studio in order to find specific scriptural references he cannot immediately locate in his Bible, not to call up passages he would not have considered otherwise. He has learned biblical truth through years of Bible study without the aid of Bible software. The searching capacities are helpful, however, when he needs to locate the exact chapter and verse for a caller. Of course, even this use of the technology could lead to laziness in memorizing the content and location of the Scriptures.

When we let computers do the intellectual work for us, we degrade ourselves before the machines we have made. Computers are becoming "smarter" while humans are dumbing down. Langdon Winner has pointed out the paradox that as "information-processing machines are becoming more 'intelligent' by leaps and bounds, much of the world's population appears to be moving in the opposite direction."[11] The decline in educational achievement in the United States has generated a number of jeremiads and lamentations along with "a blitz of electronic information, spreading computers throughout the schools, in hope that this would provide a remedy."[12] Nevertheless there is little sign that these technologies, in and of themselves, will rectify the intellectual laziness either in our schools or in our churches. On the contrary, the impressive capabilities of computers can serve to atrophy the God-given intelligence of those who use the machines.

An author I know was told by her publisher to reduce the size of her final manuscript because her revisions had increased the manuscript by almost one-third its original size. After scrupulously checking the facts of the matter, the author protested that she had added no more than 5 percent to the total, so perhaps the final count should be rechecked. The publisher responded that the count was correct since the calculation had been done entirely by computer. Postman captures the problem here:

> Because of its seeming intelligence and impartiality, a computer has an almost magical tendency to direct attention away from the people in charge of bureaucratic functions and toward itself, as if the computer were the true source of authority. . . . I am constantly amazed at how obediently people accept explanations that begin with the words "The computer shows . . ." or "The computer has determined. . . ." It is [the] equivalent of the sentence "It is God's will," and the effect is roughly the same.[13]

CYBERSPACE EVANGELISM

Because of its vast worldwide connections, some Christians see cyberspace as a wonderful opportunity to present and defend the gospel. This opportunity, however, is another two-edged sword. Electronic bulletin boards, chat rooms, and e-mail can be used to articulate the Christian worldview only if the established "netiquitte" of such forums are respected and the intrinsic limitations of the medium are recognized. Researcher Eric Pement recommends some pointers: First, before posting a message read the various message areas thoroughly because they often have set rules. Online thoughtlessness is no way to bear witness to Christ. Second, stick to the subject matter addressed in the various bulletin boards. Bombing bulletin boards with Christian messages where they are not welcome—the equivalent of digital graffiti—is plainly wrong. Third, leave short messages because readers will often not have enough patience for a long message. Fourth, refrain from posting anything representing the Christian position that is not biblical, well-reasoned, and well-written.[14]

When entering cyberspace in the above ways, we should never forget the conditions of sentience with which we are involved. Because of its disembodied, impermanent, and largely impersonal nature, cyberspace is not the best setting in which to explain or argue for the Christian message, although interaction that has begun online may lead to more engaging encounters person-to-person. Pement notes that public bulletin board service "combined sensitively with private meetings (Gal. 2:2), has already yielded many genuine conversions."[15]

The situation in which we discuss spiritual things is crucially important, as E. Stanley Jones notes with respect to the round-table discussions he held as a missionary:

> The deepest things of religion need a sympathetic atmosphere. . . . In order to discover what is most delicate and fine in religion there must be an attitude of spiritual openness, of inward sensitiveness to the Divine, a willingness to be led by the beckoning of spiritual facts.[16]

Because many things about cyberspace tend to be at odds with a sympathetic atmosphere, we must be wary in using it. When the Internet is the only way to transmit important information to a particular place, however, it should be used to the fullest. If I cannot discuss the resurrection of Christ with a Russian skeptic face-to-face, I will relish the opportunity to interact with him via cyberspace.

SEMINARIES IN CYBERSPACE?

There is a strong temptation to dumb down before "smart" technologies when educational institutions, Christian or otherwise, begin to put their classes "online." Several seminaries now advertise themselves as pioneers in cyberspace, offering "distance learning" through online classes, augmented by CD-ROMs and other home-study materials. The selling point is that students need not leave home to come to seminary. Students can learn at home at their own pace—and not disrupt anything in the process. One can learn from the best teachers without ever having to meet them. This attempt to educate the soul through cyberspace is ill-conceived for several reasons.

First, if the trend takes hold, thousands of professors may find themselves out of work, having been replaced by "better teachers" (meaning media superstars in many cases) who are squirted through cyberspace to be displayed on screens around the world. Given the tight job situation in academia, this does not bode well for a great number of talented people who have invested years of their lives and thousands of dollars in their education only to be replaced by superstars on software.

Discussions of "virtual universities" and "virtual classrooms" often neglect or suppress this bread-and butter dimension. EDUCOM, a consortium of six hundred universities and more than a hundred corporations advocating the virtual campus, predicts that when interactive multimedia become prevalent in education, students will dispense with professors entirely. Lecture courses will become extinct, being replaced by e-mail tutorials. Rather than "the sage on the stage," teachers will become "the guide at the side" through the computer. EDUCOM effuses that these technologies will reach more students and require fewer teachers. Maybe so. It would also reduce the value of education tremendously.[17]

Second, the superstars who teach these cyberclasses may be popular and charismatic without being good teachers in the full-orbed sense. Some of the greatest teachers have failed to publish voluminously or to develop a national following. Some even lack charisma. To our knowledge, Jesus wrote nothing (except in the sand) and started with a very small and unimpressive following. Socrates wrote nothing. But the unsung professor's students—the ones discipled soul-to-soul for several years—are immeasurably enriched through their professor's personal presence and dedication to truth. When education goes online it tends to go offtrack simply because the interpersonal dynamic is either lost or diminished.

One seminary advertises that it can "help you complete your degree in a way which does not disrupt your family, ministry, or lifestyle." You can "use your computer screen to access . . . the world's first full service Bible college and seminary Forum which enables students, faculty, and alumni to dialogue" as members of the school's "global community."

But seminaries have traditionally "disrupted" students' lives, and for good reason. To prepare for ministry, one must immerse oneself in biblical exegesis, theology, apologetics, ethics, practical ministry, and more. This requires a shift in one's whole life. Those called by God, however, will prevail under the demands as they labor to be men and women ready to present the gospel to a needy world. On the seminary's nonvirtual campus, students can be part of a community as they interact with professors, meet students, do internships, and spend time in the library (with walls). The "virtual seminary" suffers from many of the problems of "virtual community" discussed in chapters eight and nine. Nevertheless, one such institution proclaims that: "The Education is Real. Your Classroom Can be in Cyberspace." But there is no classroom in cyberspace, only disembodied information.

As a seminary professor, I cannot translate myself into a CD-ROM or hope to influence souls in cyberspace the way I can in the classroom. No matter how "interactive" the CD-ROM may be, there is only one conscious agent involved at any one time. Human interaction at the deepest level involves at least two participants who acknowledge and respond to each other's spoken questions, comments, and exclamations as well as the nonverbal language of embodied articulation—the raised eyebrow, the squinting eye, the furrowed brow, the misty eyes, the nodding or shaking of the head. These irreducibly personal factors and many others—such as spontaneity and humor—make up a conversation, a dialogue, in which no machine can participate.[18]

The classroom encourages serendipity, the kind of intellectual spark of discovery that is the vital life of education. I can often sense whether or not my students are comprehending the material, what bothers them, what bores them, and what excites them. I can stop for prayer whenever it seems right. I can put a student on the spot and ask him if he has done the reading when he asks a question that reveals that he has not. I can play the role of a New Ager or an atheist or a relativist in my philosophy classes to find out whether the students know how to engage these worldviews intellectually.

This kind of laboratory of the mind cannot be programmed or simulated; it can only be experienced as souls gather to seek and sift the truth. Although Paul wrote a detailed epistle to the Christians in Rome, he wanted a more personal touch: "I long to see you so that I may impart to you some spiritual gift to make you strong—that is, that you and I may be mutually encouraged by each other's faith."[19]

Paul realized that there are some crucial spiritual transactions that are not possible from a distance.

Putting theological material online and in CD-ROM format, however, does not undermine an embodied personalism so long as it does not detract from the human dynamic of learning. If a student in one seminary needs information available from a professor at a distant seminary, acquiring this material online is constructive and appropriate, provided the transaction does not impair the student's relationships with her own professors on campus.

In their zeal to acquire and disseminate biblical truth, Christians should be aware of the benefits and detriments of the technologies at their disposal. Every message—biblical or otherwise—is affected by its medium. Finding the appropriate conditions of sentience for the communication of the Christian worldview should be an ongoing challenge to those committed to representing the Word of God faithfully.

CONCLUSION

ELOQUENT REALITIES

TO USE TWO POPULAR TERMS from cyberculture, my treatment of the soul in cyberspace has been neither a rant nor a rave—although it may include more rant than rave. Perhaps the word *reflection* best describes my efforts. Given the present tendency to worship technology, some negativity is necessary in order to bring some balance. In this sense, being negative is positive.[1] The raving digitopians are easily blinded by the power of their machines; they tend to equate power and speed with moral and social improvements. The two, however, are neither equivalent nor correlative. A world-class athlete may not know how to be a loyal friend, however impressive his strength, ability, and muscular development. A cyberspace technology—such as hypertext—may dazzle, amaze, yet fail to ennoble. Wonderment is not necessarily the same as betterment. As we use the new technologies, we should employ several principles of discernment—which are neither digitopian nor Luddite.

LUDDITE INSIGHTS FOR CYBERSPACE

My reflections on cyberspace should not be taken as those of a modern day Luddite—that is, one who wants to smash the machines so to restore a better society, as did the original Luddites during the earlier stages of the industrial revolution in England. The Luddites were correct to observe, however, that some new technologies lowered wages, eliminated jobs, and displaced families. They did not oppose all technologies, but only those that affected them adversely. Some of today's critics of technology, such as revisionist author Kirkpatrick Sale, extol the Luddites and reject Western civilization entirely in favor of tribal

155

animism.[2] These extremists dismiss the idea of progress and glorify pagan cultures that were far from perfect and far from Christ. Others, like Theodore Roszak, identify themselves as neo-Luddites without denying that some technologies enhance human life.[3]

The Luddite insight should be pondered: technologies can displace our lives to our detriment and may wound our very souls. Thus we should keep technological developments in a larger perspective. Neil Postman advises that we be people "who admire technological ingenuity but do not think it represents the highest possible form of human attainment."[4] Some technologies should be refused; some should be accepted; all should be analyzed so as to guard against their dehumanizing and soul-sapping tendencies.

For instance, the sheer complexity of computer technologies can vex the soul of the nonspecialist repeatedly. (I speak from experience.) Ironically, although cyberspace is lauded as the medium to connect the world and facilitate a new era of global communications, the computers themselves are often stubbornly mute with respect to their malfunctions. Just as a baby or a pet cannot tell you what is wrong with it, computer systems can startle, perplex, and enrage their operators by bizarre messages, frozen screens, and mysterious breakdowns beyond the comprehension of most computer users. When these technologies are working properly, they can further many kinds of needful communication between people. But when they run amuck, all communication between machine and human ceases.[5]

The digitopians claim that, despite a few glitches, technological change is inevitable and ultimately desirable. We must bless the inevitable, because, after all, "you can't turn back the clock" (a phrase that usually stops all intelligent thought). But if the clock is running too quickly, it must be adjusted to match reality. Metaphors, in themselves, prove nothing; they can be twisted in any number of directions. The simple realization that what is newer may be neither truer nor better should drive us to a deeper level of analysis with respect to our culture and our worldview.

FAULTY WORLDVIEWS

Many critics of cyberspace do not have a Christian worldview. Generally speaking, they either hide their worldview, embrace Eastern forms of thought, or adhere to naturalism or postmodernism. Although some of their criticisms are valid, they lack an overall perspective adequate to steer us through the troubled terrain of cyberspace. If our understanding of cyberspace is to guide us toward what is helpful and guard us from what is harmful, it needs to be grounded in a comprehensive, consistent, and cogent worldview. We must, therefore, recognize not only the errors in non-Christian assumptions but also the implications of the Christian worldview for our use and comprehension of computer technologies.

Eastern worldviews that believe all reality is One with the divine lack a transcendent and personal point of reference by which to evaluate ethically and spiritually the contours of cyberspace and the soul itself. If the ultimate reality is beyond personality and language (as Eastern pantheistic views teach), it cannot communicate truth to persons in human language. We are bereft of an authoritative word from above that addresses our deepest concerns about ultimate reality. Instead, we are thrown back on irrational intuitions and unverifiable mystical experiences, which can never be related to a living Lord.

For instance, Mark Dery favorably quotes Joseph Campbell's pantheistic remark that at the deepest part of our being "we are at one with the nondual transcendent."[6] For Campbell this pantheistic orientation eliminates fixed moral categories and justifies evil as an expression of the ultimate unitary reality. He deems both Christ and the Hindu goddess Kali (who is always depicted wearing a necklace of human skulls and chewing human flesh) as equally appropriate symbols for the divine, despite the fact that Christ died for the ones who are responsible for his death while Kali brings death and destruction.[7] Such a viewpoint cannot, of course, provide the basis for any moral evaluation of technology—or of anything else, for that matter—because the categories of good and evil are eradicated in the supposed oneness of being.[8]

Likewise, the worldview of naturalism (or philosophical materialism) lacks a transcendent deity and must attempt to find direction in the unpredictable patterns of evolution. For instance, Mark Slouka's only metaphysical argument against disembodied existence in cyberspace is that evolution thus far has been closely connected with the larger physical world. This appeal to what has supposedly happened in the past, however, places no imperative on the present or the future. Naturalistic evolution is conceived not as a moral force but merely a physical process that might take any number of directions—including the progressive replacement of the natural with the technological in cyberspace. Evolutionary theory per se offers no argument against the aspirations of the Extropians (see chapter two), who want to take evolution in an entirely different direction through the technological augmentation of the human body.

An ethic grounded in evolution alone is a contradiction in terms because there is no moral standard above the processes of evolution by which to judge it or to direct its flow. This philosophical reality makes Slouka a prophet without either God or a revelation. He, like Sven Birkerts, lives on borrowed capital he refuses to buy or own.[9] Followers of Christ and lovers of the Scriptures, in contrast, can appropriate all the riches of biblical revelation for our intellectual discernment and practical engagement.

EMBODIED PERSONALISM

As we saw in chapter two, biblical theology and spirituality are inseparably connected to embodied personal relationships; therefore, any cyberspace technology that erodes these relationships must be rejected or held in check. When a personal encounter is impossible, cyberspace technologies can connect people otherwise inaccessible to each other. The story of the Chinese student with her mysterious illness illustrates this point (see chapter three). Western doctors could not visit her, but her medical condition could be accurately described and conveyed on the Internet. In cases like this, electronic communication does not replace an embodied encounter, since that encounter would not otherwise have happened.

Nevertheless, some fear that as medical technology becomes more sophisticated, physicians will become increasingly detached from their flesh-and-blood patients and defer to the diagnoses their machines have made. Many are now advocating that diagnoses be made from a distance, through photographs and medical information sent over the Internet. But no computer-assisted diagnosis will ever reveal the holistic state of the embodied person, that mysterious interaction of mind and body. The most objective assessment of the physical state cannot capture the subjective condition of the ailing person.[10]

I have participated in a regular e-mail conversation with a believer who is struggling through a variety of spiritual issues. As he lives across the country, our time online is not substituting for time that would otherwise be spent face-to-face—although we also converse over the telephone. I have also tried to help him find local friends and church support, which will provide what I cannot—a pat on the back, an embrace, a smile, or a look of concern, enthusiasm, or compassion.

Several years ago I heard a television preacher say that his media ministry was "discipling people" over television. I balked at this. It is possible to inform or (more likely) entertain someone through television, but biblical discipleship requires much more. It needs an ongoing, local, embodied, two-way relationship. One cannot disciple anonymously over television. Similarly, my e-mail correspondence with questioning believers is not discipleship; it is, rather, a very incomplete way of supplying information and offering advice in textual form. I may be contributing to the overall discipleship process—as a good friend did for me through many thoughtful letters during the first year of my Christian life—but I am not providing mentorship in the full-scale sense.

Nevertheless, in some situations, cyberspace may be a primary means of human contact for a disabled person. If one's body does not allow for travel or sustained person-to-person interaction, going online to find some manner of human contact is certainly appropriate. Those shut in their homes may find some profitable connections with their church and friends through the Internet, as was the case with the Alzheimer project discussed in chapter nine. The same is true for those who are immobilized in hospitals. An e-mail from the pastor, however, will never be the equivalent of a hospital call.

Despite the irreplaceable nature of embodied spiritual community, writer Dennis Oliver claims that eventually "cybercongregations" will emerge with only online members because "potentially, all the elements of congregational life can be expressed through the Internet."[11] Amazingly, Oliver ignores the physical realities of congregational singing, communion, baptism, and much more—all of which have absolutely no virtual equivalent. This transparent folly can be stated without qualification or hesitation only because digitopian notions have become so pervasive and insidious.

Cyberspace technologies excel in communicating information faster than previously possible and in linking information between computers. In areas where speed is paramount and personal contact is irrelevant or marginal, we can embrace and endorse these technologies—so long as our involvement does not adversely affect our souls in our offline lives. Essayist Wendell Berry cautions that any new technology "should not replace or disrupt anything good that already exists, and this includes family and community relationships."[12] Philosopher Albert Borgman finds that those who "surrender their substance to hyperintelligence" (cyberspace technologies) have wounded themselves unknowingly.

> Plugged into the network of communications and computers, they seem to enjoy omniscience and omnipotence; severed from their network, they turn out to be insubstantial and discontented. They no longer command their world as persons in their own rights. Their conversation is without depth and wit; their attention is roving and vacuous; their sense of place is uncertain and fickle.[13]

SILENCE AND THE SENSIBILITIES OF CYBERSPACE

The excesses of cyberspace must be counteracted by carefully guarding the formation of one's sensibilities and taking seriously the conditions of sentience that are appropriate to varying life situations. Cyberspace speeds up the onslaught of information that crashes in upon those who live in this much-vaunted "information age." But finite and fallible beings who have yet to inherit their resurrected bodies have perceptual and intellectual limits. Max Picard underscored this a generation ago when he warned of the relationship between overstimulation and superficiality. One who neglects the resources of silence will become oppressed

> by the all-too-many things that crowd in upon him every moment of his life today. He cannot be indifferent to the fact that new things are being presented to him every moment, since he must somehow enter into relationship with them. . . . When too many objects crowd in upon him and he has within no silent substance into which a part at least of this multitude of objects can disappear, the resources of emotion and passion which he has at his disposal are insufficient to meet and respond to all the objects. The

objects then lie all around him menacingly and without a proper home.[14]

One of the pervasive lies of cyberspace culture is that increased exposure to information is, in itself, good for individuals and for society as a whole. As a recent AT&T television advertisement proclaimed in breathless tones, "When people communicate, there is no limit to what they can do." AT&T was taking a page from the biblical story of the Tower of Babel for this advertisement. When the people of the world were building "a tower that reaches to the heavens," God stopped their God-defying project by confusing their language so they could not communicate with one another.[15] Digitopians today believe that communication technologies can reverse this act of God and remove all limits from what humans are able to accomplish. The communication of information has become a modern idol, rendering the God of the Bible irrelevant.[16]

But communication per se is no panacea. We may be communicating lies or half-truths or mere information without depth, breadth, or meaning. Only as we integrate information wisely into the overall context of our lives will it help us to prosper. This task is impossible without time away from the computer and other external stimulations. As Picard counsels, we need the place of silence in order to reflect on what truly matters, to set our priorities, and to respond rightly to our daily activities.[17]

A life absorbed in ceaseless stimulation is a life of superficial reaction, stress, and wasted energies. As the Preacher of Ecclesiastes pointed out, it is also an irreverent life. In his admonition not to make rash vows before the Lord, he says:

> Do not be quick with your mouth,
>> do not be hasty in your heart
>> to utter anything before God.
> God is in heaven
>> and you are on earth,
>> so let your words be few.
> As a dream comes when there are many cares,
>> so the speech of a fool when there are many words.[18]

Not being "hasty in your heart" to communicate comes from the conviction that everyone's words are uttered before the presence of a holy and all-powerful God. Jesus said, "For by your words you will be acquitted, and by your words you will be condemned."[19] Without times of reflection, meditation, prayer, silence, and solitude—unplugged and unwired moments—we lack the interior resources to govern our tongues, keyboards, and screens so that our words and lives will edify those around us and honor our Creator. Without the soul's sustained immersion in truth, we lack the resources to digest or dispense information wisely. We are embodied persons who need direction, wisdom, and renewal from a personal God.

BEING "IRISH" IN CYBERSPACE

In his delightful book *How the Irish Saved Civilization*, Thomas Cahill notes that in one of the great untold stories of history, the Irish people served civilization by preserving much of classical culture while it was being destroyed by the barbarians sacking Rome early in the fifth century. As the invaders demolished libraries, jeopardizing the wisdom of the classical world, the newly Christianized Irish saved and copied manuscripts and developed a deep love for the written word.[20]

The call to the church today is to be "Irish" in the sense of preserving and furthering spheres of truth and meaning that are threatened by technology. Today we are imperiled not by the primitives but by the moderns and postmoderns. As the technowizards spin their charms and hordes follow in mesmerized amazement, much is in jeopardy of destruction.

Hyperrealities—those technologically generated and manipulated images that correspond to no underlying reality—threaten to overwhelm the stuff of God's good creation. More people are approaching real life as though it were a video game; they are viewing people as data clusters, forgetting their own souls in favor of endless technological augmentations and amusements. In many cases, as Max Frisch notes, technology is seen as "the knack of so arranging the world that we don't have to experience it."[21] Our souls will be cheapened, neglected, or lost through the enchantments of cyberspace if we exchange electronic circuitry for the messy and wonderful world of landscapes, mountains, clouds, animals, and human beings. As Stoll says, "No computer can teach what a walk through a pine forest is like. Sensation has no substitute."[22]

Albert Borgmann warns that our immersion in cyberspace technologies may replace our involvement with what he calls "eloquent reality," realities such as horse riding, rock climbing, going to the theater or a concert, playing a musical instrument, singing in a choir, playing or attending a softball game, taking communion, enjoying a well-prepared meal or conversation with friends.[23] The unscheduled pause for reflection in the middle of a Spirit-led sermon is an eloquent reality, as is the "Amen" voiced by appreciative members of the congregation after a preacher's telling point. These events focus on the largely unmediated physical world in aesthetically and personally involving ways. Eloquent realities cannot be programmed, and they neither involve nor allow simulation.

Long before cyberspace was even a word, Ben Hecht wrote a story about the jamming of the world's airwaves by mysterious extraterrestrial sources. People were faced with a startling silence. Despite the dismay of some who could not endure the absence of constant noise, there was an "improvement in the mood of the world" because eloquent realities had returned.

> The return of music to the theaters and auditoriums has brought that oldest art back to itself. And there has been restored to man, particularly the workingman, whose leisure hours are precious, some measure of reflection. A sort of peace has descended on Earth. In the very first spring following the miracle many strange and unheard-of things began to happen. People picked flowers again, sat in the grass, read books and poems, or let their hands lie idle in the sun.[24]

Getting unplugged and reintegrated into God's world of eloquent realities may help remind us that "the heavens declare the glory of God,"[25] and that the Creator's eternal power and divine nature are revealed in the universe he designed and brought forth.[26] Removing ourselves for a time from our own creations may allow us to remember that we ourselves are creatures who are "fearfully and wonderfully made,"[27] bearing the image and likeness of God.

Even without Luddites from the skies to disconnect us forcibly, we may experience "unheard-of things" when we discipline our souls and our technologies to obey the Lord of heaven and earth. Like the Christian Irish of old, we must intentionally conserve much of great value that would be lost if we were to thrust our souls into cyberspace without a second thought. The fact that we are all immortal beings who will one day be resurrected to eternal glory or eternal infamy should cause us to ponder how any technology will affect our own destiny and that of others. As C. S. Lewis famously noted a generation ago,

> It is a serious thing to live in a society of possible gods and goddesses, to remember that the dullest and most uninteresting person you can talk to may one day be a creature which, if you saw it now, you would be strongly tempted to worship, or else a horror and a corruption such as you now meet, if at all, only in a nightmare. All day long we are, in some degree, helping each other to one or other of these destinations. It is in the light of these overwhelming possibilities, it is with the awe and the circumspection proper to them, that we should conduct all our dealings with one another, all friendships, all loves, all law, all politics.[28]

And it is in light of these overwhelming possibilities that we should conduct all our dealings with this strange new world of cyberspace.

NOTES

Introduction: Cyberspace and the Trouble with our Souls

1. *Denver Post,* 4 July 1995.
2. Nicholas Negroponte, *Being Digital* (New York: Alfred A. Knopf, 1995), 7.
3. Cited in Clifford Stoll, *Silicon Snake Oil: Second Thoughts on the Information Highway* (New York: Doubleday, 1995), 21.
4. "50 and 100 Years Ago," *Scientific American,* June 1994, 12.
5. Quoted in *The New York Times Magazine,* 3 March 1996, 40.
6. This will be addressed in more depth in chapter eight.
7. William J. Bennett, *The Index of Cultural Indicators* (New York: NY: Touchstone, 1994), 8; emphasis in the original.
8. Eugene Taylor, "Desperately Seeking Spirituality," *Psychology Today,* November/December 1994, 55ff.
9. For more on the new spirituality, see Douglas Groothuis, *Jesus in an Age of Controversy* (Eugene, OR: Harvest House, 1996), 64–76.
10. Steven Levy, "The Year of the Internet," *Newsweek,* 25 December 1995–1 January 1996, 25.
11. For a detailed account of this see Howard Rheingold, *The Virtual Community: Homesteading on the Electronic Frontier* (Reading, MA: Addison-Wesley, 1993), 65–109.
12. Levy, 26.
13. See Bill Gates with Nathan Myhrvold and Peer Rinearson, *The Road Ahead* (New York: Viking, 1995).
14. Neil Postman, *The End of Education: Redefining the Value of School* (New York: Alfred A. Knopf, 1995), 38.
15. Langdon Winner, *The Whale and the Reactor* (Chicago: The University of Chicago Press, 1986), 10.
16. Ibid., 5.
17. Ibid., 9.

18. Cited in Kirkpatrick Sale, *Rebels Against the Future: The Luddites and their War on the Industrial Revolution* (Reading, MA: Addison-Wesley, 1995), 209.

19. Neil Postman, *Technopoly: The Surrender of Culture to Technology* (New York: Alfred A. Knopf, 1992), 18. On the pervasive effects of television see Neil Postman, *Amusing Ourselves to Death: Public Discourse in the Age of Show Business* (New York: Penguin, 1985).

20. This has been an ongoing theme in the work of Jacques Ellul. See especially, *The Technological Society* (New York: Vintage Books, 1964), *The Technological System* (New York: Continuum, 1980), and *The Technological Bluff* (Grand Rapids, MI: Eerdmans, 1990).

21. We will say much more about this in chapter three.

22. Quoted in Dinah Wisenberg Brin, "Ice Cream Truck Driver Killed in Robbery, 16-Year-Old Arrested," Associated Press report (17 June 1994); cited in Lynne V. Cheney, *Telling the Truth: Why Our Culture and Our Country Have Stopped Making Sense—and What We Can Do About It* (New York: Simon and Schuster, 1995), 203–4.

23. John Whalen, "Super Searcher," Interview with Reva Basch, *Wired*, May 1995, 153.

24. Max Picard, *The World of Silence*, trans. Stanley Godman (Chicago: Henry Regnery, 1952), ix.

25. Ibid., 196.

26. Ibid., 198.

27. Sale, 265.

28. Picard, 201.

29. Ibid.

30. Ibid., 206.

31. Romans 12:2. See also 1 John 2:15–17.

32. Matthew 5:13.

33. See Exodus 20:1–17; Matthew 5:1–12; 1 Corinthians 13:1–3; Galatians 5:19–23.

34. Francis A. Schaeffer, *The God Who Is There: Speaking Historic Christianity into the Twentieth Century* (Downers Grove, IL: InterVarsity Press, 1968), 18; emphasis in the original.

35. 1 Chronicles 12:32.

36. Jacques Ellul, *In Season, Out of Season* (San Francisco, CA: Harper and Row, 1982), 106.

37. Blaise Pascal, *Pensées*, trans. A. J. Krailsheimer (New York: Penguin, 1966), 699/382, p. 247.

38. The philosophy of the builders of the Tower of Babel (Genesis 11) is evident in some technological orientations, however. See chapter nine.

39. We will have more to say about Luddism in the book's conclusion.

40. Genesis 1:26–28; Psalm 8:4–9.

41. 1 Thessalonians 5:21–22.

Chapter 1: The Postmodern Soul in Cyberspace

1. *The Letters of Marshall McLuhan,* Matie Molinaro, Corinne McLuhan, and William Toyes, eds. (New York: Oxford University Press, 1987), 309.
2. G. K. Chesterton, *Orthodoxy* (Garden City, NY: Image Books, 1959), 54.
3. Blaise Pascal, *Pensées,* trans. A. J. Krailsheimer (New York: Penguin, 1966), 75/389, p. 49.
4. Mark Slouka, *War of the Worlds: Cyberspace and the High-Tech Assault on Reality* (New York: Basic Books, 1995), 56–60.
5. To be specific, a MOO refers to a MUD whose programming is object-oriented.
6. See Robert Rossney, "Metaworlds," *Wired,* June 1996, 142ff.
7. Sherry Turkle, *Life on the Screen: Identity in the Age of Internet* (New York: Simon and Schuster, 1995), 11.
8. Slouka, 59–60.
9. Ibid., 59.
10. Ibid., 60.
11. Kenneth Gergen, "The Healthy, Happy Human Being Wears Many Masks," in *The Truth About Truth: De-confusing and Re-constructing the Postmodern World,* ed. Walter Truit Anderson (New York: J/P/ Tarcher/Putman, 1995), 144.
12. James 1:8; see also 4:8.
13. For an excellent summary of this historical and philosophical development, see Os Guinness, *The Dust of Death: The Sixties Counter-culture and How It Changed America Forever* (Wheaton, IL: Crossway Books, 1994), 17–52. The chapter is appropriately called "The Striptease of Humanism."
14. Benjamin Woolley, *Virtual Worlds* (New York: Penguin Books, 1992), 169.
15. Turkle, 49. Turkle is speaking primarily of the work of Fredrick Jameson.
16. Ibid., 49.
17. Thomas Moore, *Care of the Soul: A Guide for Cultivating Depth and Sacredness in Everyday Life* (New York: HarperPerennial, 1992), 99, 107, 233.
18. Ibid., 246.
19. Peter Berger, *A Far Glory: The Quest for Faith in an Age of Credulity* (New York: Dell Publishing Group, 1992), 98.
20. Pascal, 697/383, p. 247.
21. Pamela McCorduck, "Sex, Lies, and Avatars," Interview with Sherry Turkle, *Wired,* April 1996, 164.
22. Ibid.
23. Ibid., 165.
24. See Genesis 3; Romans 3.
25. Michael Heim, *The Metaphysics of Virtual Reality* (New York: Oxford University Press, 1993), 133.

26. For a summary and critique of Taoism see Kent Kedl and Dean C. Halverson, "Taoism," in *The Compact Guide to World Religions*, ed. Dean Halverson (Minneapolis, MN: Bethany House, 1995), 216–233.
27. See Gergen, 138–142.
28. William James, *The Varieties of Religious Experience: The Words of William James*, ed. Frederick Burkhardt (Cambridge: Harvard University Press, 1985), 400. For an argument against the view that all religions teach the same reality, see Douglas Groothuis, *Are All Religions One?* (Downers Grove, IL: InterVarsity Press, 1996).
29. Chesterton, 158.
30. Pascal, 149/430, p. 77.
31. Gergen, 143; emphasis in the original.
32. Berger, 122.
33. 1 Timothy 2:5.
34. On the biblical and reformed doctrine of justification by faith alone, see R. C. Sproul, *Faith Alone* (Grand Rapids, MI: Baker Books, 1995).
35. Mark 7:21–23.
36. Psalm 86:11.
37. Galatians 5:22–23.
38. Galatians 5:19–21.
39. See 1 Corinthians 12-14; Romans 14; Ephesians 4:11–13; 1 Peter 4:10–11.
40. Frederick Buechner, *Wishful Thinking: A Theological ABC* (New York: Harper and Row, 1973), 95. For an excellent treatment of the biblical doctrine of calling, see Os Guinness, "The Calling of God," audio tape available from Trinity Forum Publishing, 5210 Lyngate Court, Suite B, Burke, VA 22015; and John Stott, *The Contemporary Christian: Applying God's Word to Today's World* (Downers Grove, IL: InterVarsity Press, 1992), 128–145.

Chapter 2: Disembodied Existence in a Digital World

1. For a brief overview of the angel phenomenon, see Douglas Groothuis, *Jesus in an Age of Controversy* (Eugene, OR: Harvest House, 1996), 288–90.
2. Albert Borgman, *Crossing the Postmodern Divide* (Chicago: University of Chicago Press, 1992), 105.
3. Ibid.
4. Dan Pacheco, "Health on the 'Net: A Place to Flee From Phobias," *Denver Post*, 6 December 1994, 2E.
5. Ibid.
6. William Irwin Thompson, *The American Replacement of Nature: The Everyday Acts and Outrageous Evolution of Economic Life* (New York: Doubleday, 1991). Thompson is a pantheist.
7. Ibid., 17–79; see also Jacques Ellul, *The Technological Bluff* (Grand Rapids, MI: Eerdmans, 1990), 381–82.

8. Quoted in Kevin Kelly, *Out of Control: The New Biology of Machines, Social Systems, and the Economic World* (Reading, MA: Addison-Wesley, 1994), 349–350.

9. On this see J. P. Moreland, ed. *The Design Hypothesis: Scientific Evidence for Intelligent Design* (Downers Grove, IL: InterVarsity Press, 1994).

10. Compare Luke 18:27; see also Romans 9:20.

11. Quoted in Mark Dery, *Escape Velocity: Cyberculture at the End of the Century* (New York: Grove Press, 1996), 260.

12. William Gibson, *Neuromancer* (New York: Ace Books, 1984), 6; quoted in Michael Heim, *The Metaphysics of Virtual Reality* (New York: Oxford University Press, 1994), 102.

13. Hans Moravec, *Mind Children: The Future of Robot and Human Intelligence* (Cambridge: Harvard University Press, 1988), 6.

14. See Theodore Roszak, *The Cult of Information: A Neo-Luddite Treatise on High-Tech, Artificial Intelligence, and the True Art of Thinking*, revised edition (Berkeley, CA: University of California Press, 1994), xii.

15. Moravec, 110.

16. Ibid., 112.

17. Ibid., 114.

18. Dery, 302.

19. David Ross, "Persons, Programs, and Uploading Consciousness," *Extropy* 4, no. 1 (9), 14; quoted in Dery, 301.

20. Dery, 302.

21. For a critique of the Extropians from a Christian perspective, see Brian Godawa, "Extropianism: Techno-Anarchy for a Brave New World," *SCP Journal*, 19:4–20:1 (1995), 36–45.

22. G. K. Chesterton, *Generally Speaking* (New York: Dodd, Mead and Co., 1929), 14; quoted in *The Quotable Chesterton: A Topical Compilation of the Wit, Wisdom, and Satire of G.K. Chesterton*, eds. George J. Marlin, Richard P. Rabatin, and John L. Swan (Garden City: New York, 1987), 213.

23. I take this up in more depth in chapter five.

24. Much more can be said on the classic mind-body problem in philosophy. For a good overview see the chapter "The Argument From Mind" in J. P. Moreland, *Scaling the Secular City* (Grand Rapids, MI: Baker Books, 1987). Theodore Roszak also argues against reducing the human mind to a computer or viewing computers as having real intelligence in *The Cult of Information: A Neo-Luddite Treatise on High-Tech, Artificial Intelligence, and the True Art of Thinking*, second edition (Berkeley, CA: University of California Press, 1994). Roszak's worldview, however, is pantheistic.

25. C. S. Lewis, *The Screwtape Letters* (New York: Macmillan, 1982), 33.

26. Mark Slouka, *War of The Worlds: Cyberspace and the High-Tech Assault on Reality* (New York: Basic Books, 1995), 20.

27. Jeffrey Meyers, *D.H. Lawrence* (New York: Alfred A. Knopf, 1993), 363; quoted in Dery, 236.

28. Genesis 1; John 1:1–4.
29. Genesis 2:7.
30. Psalm 139:14.
31. See Romans 1–3.
32. John 1:14.
33. Galatians 4:4.
34. Philippians 2:6–11.
35. Colossians 2:9.
36. Colossians 1:21–22.
37. 1 Timothy 4:3–4; see also Colossians 2:20–23.
38. See Daniel 12:1–2.
39. See Philippians 1: 21–24; 2 Corinthians 5:1–10; 1 Thessalonians 4:13–18.
40. Acts 1:3.
41. 1 Corinthians 15:20–23. For historical arguments for the resurrection of Christ, see Douglas Groothuis, *Jesus in an Age of Controversy* (Eugene, OR: Harvest House, 1996), 272–82.
42. See Romans 8:19–21; Revelation 21.
43. 2 John 12.
44. 3 John 13–14.
45. 1 John 1:1.
46. Galatians 2:9.
47. Romans 16:16; see also 1 Peter 5:14.
48. Acts 28:8; 2 Timothy 1:6.
49. Heim, 102.
50. For an explanation of an evangelical, egalitarian view, see Rebecca Merrill Groothuis, *Women Caught in the Conflict: The Culture War Between Traditionalism and Feminism* (Grand Rapids, MI: Baker Books, 1994) and Rebecca Merrill Groothuis, *Good News for Women: A Biblical Picture of Gender Equality* (Grand Rapids, MI: Baker Books, 1997).
51. For an interesting discussion of the advantages of traditional mail over e-mail, see Clifford Stoll, *Silicon Snake Oil: Second Thoughts on the Information Highway* (New York: Doubleday, 1995), 160–66.
52. 1 Kings 3:1–15.

Chapter 3: The Book, the Screen, and the Soul

1. See Genesis 3.
2. Malcolm McConnell, "Rescue on the Internet," *Reader's Digest,* August 1996, 42. The woman's information can be found at: http://www.radsci.ucla.edu/telemed/zhuling.
3. We will address this issue briefly in the conclusion. One helpful web site for medical information is Medline: http://www.healthgate.com.
4. Jason Baker, *The Christian Cyberspace Companion* (Grand Rapids, MI: Baker Books, 1995).

5. See Jacques Ellul, *The Technological Bluff* (Grand Rapids, MI: Eerdmans, 1990), 73–76.
6. Romans 8:20–22.
7. Proverbs 14:12, NRSV.
8. Proverbs 18:17.
9. This is a variation on the term "arena of sentience" used by Sven Birkerts who participated in the discussion, "What Are We Doing On-Line?" *Harpers*, August 1995, 39.
10. Sven Birkerts, *The Gutenberg Elegies* (Boston: Faber and Faber, 1994), 122.
11. William H. Gass, "The Book as Container of Consciousness," *Wilson Quarterly*, Winter 1995, 91.
12. Birkerts, 87.
13. We will return to this in more depth in the conclusion.
14. Simon Weil, *Gravity and Grace* (New York: Routledge, 1992), 106.
15. Hebrews 5:13–14, NRSV.
16. Matthew 6:22–23.
17. Neil Postman, *Amusing Ourselves to Death: Public Discourse in the Age of Show Business* (New York: Penguin Books, 1985), 63.
18. Quoted in John Leo, "Spicing Up the (Ho-Hum) Truth," *U.S. News and World Report*, March 8, 1993, 24. On the anti-intellectual effects of television, see also Tom Shachtman, *The Inarticulate Society: Eloquence and Culture in America* (New York: Free Press, 1995), especially 99–152.
19. Charles Krauthammer, "Printing on Way Out, Writing's Not," *Rocky Mountain News* 24 June, 1996, 31A.
20. Quoted in D.T. Max, "The End of the Book?" *Atlantic Monthly*, September 1994, 68; emphasis mine.
21. Exodus 32:15–16.
22. Exodus 34:1–28.
23. Revelation 1:19.
24. Erik Ness, "The Fate of Fiction in the Electronic Age," *Isthmus* (12 January 12 1996), 21.
25. Birkerts, 157.
26. Michael Heim, *The Metaphysics of Virtual Reality* (New York: Oxford University Press, 1994), 5.
27. Clifford Stoll, *Silicon Snake Oil* (New York: Doubleday, 1995), 26.
28. Ibid., 25.
29. Theodore Rozsak, *The Cult of Information: A Neo-Luddite Treatise on High-Tech, Artificial Intelligence, and the True Art of Thinking*, revised edition (Berkeley, CA: University of California Press, 1994), 193.
30. See Stoll, 176.
31. Benjamin Woolley, *Virtual Worlds* (New York: Penguin, 1992), 158.
32. Ibid., 160.
33. Gary Wolf, "The Curse of Xanadu," *Wired*, June 1995, 137.
34. Jeff Rothenberg, "Ensuring the Longevity of Digital Documents," *Scientific American*, January 1995, 45.

35. I have adjusted the spelling slightly.
36. Rothenberg, 42.
37. Stoll, 180.
38. Rothenberg, 42.
39. Ibid., 42.
40. Roszak, 194.
41. Ibid., 196.
42. Quoted in Max, 71.
43. Ibid.
44. Ibid.
45. Compare this with Isaiah 40:8 and Matthew 5:18.
46. Stoll, 182.
47. John Milton, *Areopagitica*, in *The Prose of John Milton*, ed. J. Max Patrick (New York, 1968), 271; quoted in Gertrude Himmelfarb, *On Looking Into the Abyss: Untimely Thoughts on Culture and Society* (New York: Vintage Books, 1994), 98.
48. Stoll gives a fascinating and convincing argument for the superiority of card catalogs over computer search techniques. See Stoll, 197–203.

Chapter 4: Hypertext Realities and Effects

1. See Michael Heim, *The Metaphysics of Virtual Reality* (New York: Oxford University Press, 1994), 30.
2. Neil Postman and Camille Paglia, "She Wants Her TV! He wants His Book!" *Harpers*, March 1991, 54.
3. From Christmas of 1993 to Christmas of 1995, the number of consumers who owned CD-ROMs jumped from fewer than nine million to an estimated forty million. Seventeen million purchases were expected in 1996. [Paul Roberts, "Virtual Grub Street," *Harpers*, June 1996, 72.]
4. Jacques Ellul, *The Humiliation of the Word* (Grand Rapids, MI: Eerdmans, 1985).
5. Roberts, 77.
6. Ellul, 133.
7. John Whalen, "Super Searcher," Interview with Reva Basch, *Wired*, May 1995, 153.
8. Cited in Stephen Carter, *Integrity* (New York: Basic Books, 1996), 28.
9. Thomas Oden, *Between Two Worlds: Notes on the Death of Modernity in America and Russia* (Downers Grove, IL: InterVarsity Press, 1992), 130–31.
10. John Horgan, "The Death of Proof," *Scientific American*, October 1993, 103.
11. Richard A. Lanham, *The Electronic Word: Democracy, Technology, and the Arts* (Chicago: The University of Chicago Press, 1993), 51; quoted in Sherry Turkle, *Life on the Screen: Identity in the Age of the Internet* (New York: Simon and Schuster, 1995), 18.

12. Ibid.
13. Benjamin Woolley, *Virtual Worlds* (New York: Penguin, 1992), 153.
14. John Barth, "The State of the Art," *The Wilson Quarterly*, Spring 1996, 36.
15. Blaise Pascal, *Pensées*, trans. A. J. Krailsheimer (New York: Penguin Books, 1966), 251/900, p. 104. Pascal is commenting on Augustine's *De Doctrina Christiana*, III-27. See also 2 Peter 3:16.
16. Robert Coover, "The End of Books," *New York Times Book Review*, 21 June 21, 1992, 23.
17. Marshall McLuhan, *Understanding Media: The Extensions of Man* (McGraw-Hill, 1965), 19.
18. C. S. Lewis, *An Experiment in Criticism* (Cambridge, England: Cambridge University Press, 1961), 85. See also Bruce L. Edwards, "C. S. Lewis and the Deconstructionists," *This World* 10 (Winter 1985): 88–98.
19. Quoted (without reference) in John Stott, *Romans* (Downers Grove, IL: InterVarsity Press, 1994). Oh, for a hypertext index on Muggeridge as well!
20. Woolley, 165.
21. David Gelernter, "Unplugged," *Technos* 4, 1 (Spring 1995): 27.
22. Gary Wolf, "Channeling McLuhan: The Wired Interview with Wired's Patron Saint," *Wired*, January 1996, 129.
23. Kevin Kelly, "Gossip is Philosophy," Interview with Brian Eno, *Wired*, July 1995, 151.
24. Nicholas Negroponte, *Being Digital* (New York: Alfred A. Knopf, 1995), 224.
25. Ginia Bellafante, "Strange Sounds and Sights," *Time*, Special Issue: Welcome to Cyberspace, Spring 1995, 14.
26. Ibid.
27. Kelly, 207.
28. Friedrich Nietzsche, *Thus Spoke Zarathustra*, in *The Portable Nietzsche*, ed. Walter Kaufmann (New York: Viking, 1968), 171.
29. On this, see C. S. Lewis, *The Abolition of Man* (New York: Collier Books, 1955).
30. Coover, 26.
31. William Gibson, *Mona Lisa Overdrive* (New York: Bantam Books, 1988), 49; quoted in Heim, 81.
32. Daniel J. Boorstin, *The Image: A Guide to Pseudo-Events in America* (New York: Atheneum, 1961), 94.
33. Paul Virilio, *The Art of the Motor*, trans. Julie Rose (Minneapolis, MN: University of Minnesota Press, 1995), 131–32; emphasis in the original.
34. 2 Timothy 3:7.
35. Seneca, *Letters of Seneca*, trans. Robin Campbell (London: Penguin Books, 1969), letter 33.
36. Ibid., letter 32.

Chapter 5: The Fate of Truth in Cyberspace

1. Blaise Pascal, *Pensées*, trans. A. J. Krailsheimer (New York: Penguin Books, 1966), 739/864, p. 256.
2. Ibid., 119/423, p. 60. On this theme, see Proverbs 8.
3. Ibid., 176/261, p. 84.
4. C. S. Lewis, *The Screwtape Letters* (New York: Macmillan, 1982), 8.
5. Ibid.
6. Simone Weil, *The Need for Roots*, trans. Arthur Wills (Boston: Beacon Press, 1952), 37.
7. See Stephen Talbot, *The Future Does Not Compute: Transcending the Machines in our Midst* (Sebastopol, CA: O'Reilly and Associates, 1995), 211.
8. John 18:37.
9. Francis Bacon, *The Essays*, ed. John Pitcher (New York: Penguin Books, 1985), 61.
10. John 14:6.
11. For a defense of the correspondence view of truth and Christianity as true, see Winfried Corduan, *Reasonable Faith: Basic Christian Apologetics* (Nashville, TN: Broadman & Holman, 1993), especially chapter 2.
12. Jean Baudrillard, *Simulacra and Simulation*, trans. Sheila Faria Glaser (Ann Arbor, MI: University of Michigan Press, 1994), 79.
13. Neil Postman, *Technopoly: The Surrender of Culture to Technology* (New York: Alfred A. Knopf, 1992), 70.
14. Pascal, 723/69, p. 251.
15. This is explored in some interesting ways in Jeremy Rifkin, *Time Wars: The Primary Conflict in Human History* (New York: Simon and Schuster, 1987).
16. Michael Heim, *The Metaphysics of Virtual Reality* (New York: Oxford University Press, 1994), 10.
17. Jacques Ellul, *The Technological Bluff* (Grand Rapids, MI: Eerdmans, 1990), 330.
18. Michael Meyer, "Meaning of Life," *Virtual City*, Spring 1996, 80.
19. Pascal, 414/171, p. 148.
20. Ibid., 24/127, p. 36.
21. Ibid., 620/146, p. 235.
22. Ibid., 132/170, p. 66.
23. Ibid.
24. Ibid., 166/183, p. 82.
25. Ibid., 70/165b.
26. T. S. Eliot, *Murder in the Cathedral* (New York, NY: Harcourt, Brace, and World, 1963), 69.
27. Pascal, 148/429, p. 75.
28. Simone Weil, *Gravity and Grace*, trans. Emma Craufurd (New York: Routledge, 1992), 10.

29. Ecclesiastes 3:11.

30. Pascal, 641/129, p. 238.

31. See Marilyn Elias, "Net Overuse Called 'True Addiction'," USA Today, 1 July 1996 for the view that Internet use can become an addiction.

32. Mark Slouka, War of the Worlds: Cyberspace and the Hi-Tech Assault on Reality (New York: Basic Books, 1995), 48.

33. Steven Daly and Nathaniel Wice, alt.culture: an a-to-z guide to the '90s— underground, online, and over the counter (New York: HarperPerennial, 1995), 154.

34. Cited in Karen Coyle, "How Hard Can it Be?" Working Woman, June 1996, book excerpt, no page.

35. Quoted in Marc Laidlaw, "The Egos at Id," Wired, August 1996, 186.

36. Allucquere Rosanne Stone, The War of Desire and Technology at the Close of the Mechanical Age (Cambridge, MA: The MIT Press, 1995), 27.

37. Pascal, 551/84, 220. For a discussion of the imagination's place within a Christian worldview, see Francis A. Schaeffer, He is There, He is Not Silent (Wheaton, IL: Tyndale House, 1972), 85–87.

38. Ibid., 152/213, p. 81. I have altered the translation slightly to make it more clear.

39. Alvin and Heidi Toffler, Creating a New Civilization: The Politics of the Third Wave (Atlanta, GA: Turner Publishing, 1995), 36; emphasis added.

40. On the problems with this, see Theodore Roszak, The Cult of Information: A Neo-Luddite Treatise on Hi-Tech, Artificial Intelligence, and the True Art of Thinking, revised edition (Berkeley, CA: University of California Press, 1994), 3–16.

41. On this, see Clifford Stoll, Silicon Snake Oil: Second Thoughts on the Information Highway (New York: Doubleday, 1995), 191–96.

42. Erik Ness, "The Fate of Fiction in the Electronic Age, Isthmus 12 January 1996, 22.

43. Aleksandr I. Solzhenitsyn, A World Split Apart, trans. Irina Ilovayskaya Alberti (New York: Harper and Row 1978), 25, 27.

44. 1 Timothy 6:20.

45. Jean Baudrillard, The Transparency of Evil, trans. James Benedict (New York: Verso, 1993), 12–13.

46. Baudrillard, Simulacra and Simulation, 1.

47. Ibid., 2.

48. See Ibid., 159–164.

49. Roszak, 37.

50. Postman, 60.

51. 1 Corinthians 8:1.

52. See Ephesians 4:15.

53. Talbot, 111.

54. Postman, 80.

55. Ibid., 79.

56. Ibid., 78.

57. Sven Birkerts, *Gutenberg Elegies: The Fate of Reading in an Electronic Age* (Boston: Faber and Faber, 1994), 75.
58. Ibid., 228.
59. Ibid., 212.
60. Ibid.
61. Neil Postman, *The End of Education: Redefining the Value of School* (New York: Alfred A. Knopf, 1995), 69–70. Postman is concerned about unthinking dogmatism, but he seems to rule out any final answers to perennial questions.
62. Ibid., 11, 57, 107.
63. On this, see R. C. Sproul, *Not a Chance: The Myth of Chance in Modern Science and Cosmology* (Grand Rapids, MI: Baker Books, 1994), 72–75. On the importance of sound logic in formulating worldviews, see Ronald Nash, *Worldviews in Conflict: Choosing Christianity in a World of Ideas* (Grand Rapids, MI: Zondervan, 1992), 55–57, 80–84, 93–106, 140–43.
64. John 1:9.
65. Hebrews 6:18.
66. Colossians 2:3.
67. James 1:5; see also Proverbs 2:1–10.
68. Philippians 2:6–7.
69. Hebrews 1:2.
70. Hebrews 4:12–13.
71. Weil, 40.

Chapter 6: Cybersex: Eroticism without Bodies

1. This translation is taken from Jaroslav Pelikan, *The Melody of Theology: A Philosophical Dictionary* (Cambridge, MA: Harvard University Press, 1988), 2.
2. G. K. Chesterton, *St. Francis of Assisi* (Garden City, NY: Doubleday, 1954), 41.
3. William J. Bennett, *The Index of Leading Cultural Indicators* (New York: Simon and Schuster, 1994), 46.
4. Ibid., 47.
5. Ibid., 68.
6. Ibid., 58.
7. Ibid., 59.
8. Ibid., 50.
9. Ibid., 52–54.
10. See Ted Guest with Victoria Pope, "Crime Time Bomb," *U.S. News & World Report*, 25 March, 1996, 28–36.
11. Mark Dery, *Escape Velocity: Cyberculture at the End of the Twentieth Century* (New York: Grove Press, 1996), 199.
12. Philippians 3:19.
13. Dery, 199.

14. Ibid., 200. I have never visited such places, so I take Dery's and others' word for the descriptions that follow.
15. Ibid., 200.
16. Ibid., 200–1.
17. Ibid., 207–8
18. Ibid., 205.
19. Howard Rheingold, *The Virtual Community* (Reading, MA: Addison-Wesley, 1993), 150.
20. Ibid.
21. Sherry Turkle, *Life on Screen: Identity in the Age of Internet* (New York: Simon and Schuster, 1995), 251.
22. Anne Balsamo, "Feminism for the Incurably Informed," *Flame Wars: The Discourse of Cyberculture*, ed. Mark Dery (Durham, NC: Duke University Press, 1994), 139.
23. Turkle, 252.
24. Julian Dibbell, "A Rape in Cyberspace," *Village Voice*, 2 December, 1993, 38; quoted in Dery, 206.
25. Online interview with Sherry Turkle on "Live With Derek McGinty," May 2, 1996, at: http://www.discovery.com/DCO/doc/1012/world/tlive/chat5-2-96/logo.html.
26. Susan Margolis, "Virtual Reality Offers New Treatment of Phobias," *One Source*, Spring 1996, 11–12.
27. Dery, 211.
28. Howard Rheingold, *Virtual Reality* (New York: Summit Books, 1991), 346.
29. Ibid.
30. Jude 12.
31. See Dery, 212. Paul's statement "For it is shameful even to mention what the disobedient do in secret" (Ephesians 5:12) applies to these speculations.
32. Quoted in *Re/Search* 8/9, 157; quoted in Dery, 192.
33. See Dery, 209–10.
34. Ibid., 210.
35. Jean Baudrillard, *Simulacra and Simulation*, trans. Sheila Faria Glaser (Ann Arbor, MI: The University of Michigan Press, 1994), 2.
36. Quoted in Karen Coyle, "How Hard Can it Be?" *Working Woman*, July 1996, no page; book excerpt from Lynn Cheney and Elizabeth Reba Weise, *Wired Women: Gender and New Realities in Cyberspace* (Seattle: Seal Press, 1996).
37. Ibid.
38. Philip Elmer-Dewitt, "Cyberporn," *Time*, 3 July, 1995, 38–39.
39. Peter H. Lewis, "New Concerns Raised Over a Computer Smut Study," *New York Times*, 16 July, 1995, National section, 22; cited in Dery, 207.
40. See Thomas J. DeLoughry, "The 'Data Geeks' of the Internet," *The Chronicle of Higher Education*, 22 March 1996, 21ff.

41. Garreth Branwyn, "Wired Top 10," *Wired*, June 1996, 72. This list was compiled 12 March 1996.
42. *Internet Underground*, July 1995, 79.
43. Ibid., 77.
44. The Flogmaster, "About Spanking," *Internet Underground*, June 1996, 68.
45. Wendy Cole, "The Marquis de Cyberspace, " *Time*, 3 July 1995, 43.
46. Arianna Huffington, Cyberspace Porn Diminishes Society," *Rocky Mountain News*, 14 March 1996, 45A.
47. Romans 1:25.
48. 1 Timothy 4:1–4; Colossians 2:23.
49. Jeremiah 16:20.
50. Jeremiah 2:5.
51. Michael Heim, *The Metaphysics of Virtual Reality* (New York: Oxford University Press, 1994), 100–101.
52. Jill Smolowe, "Intimate Strangers," *Time*, Special Issue: Welcome to Cyberspace, Spring 1995, 21.
53. Matthew 5:27–28.
54. See Turkle, *Life on the Screen*, 225–26. Turkle remains amoral on these implications.
55. Matthew 22:37; John 8:31–32.
56. On the perverse powers of the imagination see Blaise Pascal, *Pensées*, trans. A. J. Krailsheimer (New York: Penguin, 1966), 44/82, p. 38–42.
57. James 1:14–15.
58. 2 Corinthians 10:5.
59. Philippians 4:8–9, NRSV.
60. Proverbs 4:23.
61. Psalm 101:3.
62. 1 John 2:15, NRSV.
63. Titus 2:11–12. I substituted "people" for "men" in verse 11.
64. 2 Corinthians 1:20.
65. E. Stanley Jones, *The Divine Yes* (Nashville, TN: Abingdon Press, 1975), 22.
66. Jacques Ellul, *What I Believe* (Grand Rapids, MI: Eerdmans Publishing Company, 1989), 82. The essay from which this quotation comes, "Life Long Love," is quite insightful in many places.
67. Simone Weil, *Gravity and Grace* trans. Emma Craufurd (New York: Routledge, 1992), 72.
68. Matthew 16:25–26, NRSV.

Chapter 7: Technoshamanism: Digital Deities

1. Quoted in Steven Daly and Nathanial Wice, *alt.culture: an a-t-z guide to the 90s—underground, online, and over-the-counter* (New York: HarperPerennial, 1995), 130.
2. Steve Ditlea, "Leary's Final Trip, the Web, Realized His Multimedia Vision," *New York Times*, 1 June, 1996; online documentation.

3. Douglas Rushkoff, *Cyberia: Life in the Trenches of Hyperspace* (New York: HarperCollins, 1994), 44–45, 49–50, 57, 61, 66, 132–33, 211, 229.
4. Ibid., 61.
5. Douglas Rushkoff, "Life at Tim's, After Tim," Timothy Leary's home page: http://www.leary.com.
6. See Mark Dery, *Escape Velocity* (New York: Grove Press, 1995), 22.
7. Timothy Leary Transcript, "Club Wired," *HotWired*, August 10, 1995, at: http://www.hotwired.com/club/special/transcripts/95-08-10.leary.html.
8. Quoted in Dery, 28. Dery is quoting from a personal interview with Leary.
9. Rushkoff, *Cyberia*, 30.
10. See Dery, 22.
11. For a short survey of this, see Stewart Brand, "We Owe it All To the Hippies," *Time*, Special Issue: Welcome to Cyberspace, Spring 1995, 54–56.
12. Ibid., 22.
13. Erik Davis, "Techgnosis, Magic, Memory, and the Angels of Information," in *Flame Wars: The Discourse of Cyberspace*, ed. Mark Dery (Duke University Press, 1994), 54–55.
14. Quoted in Rushkoff, *Cyberia*, 58. The fact that the Buddha and Jesus Christ taught entirely different things about ultimate reality, the human condition, and spiritual liberation seems to be lost on McKenna.
15. Quoted in Ibid., 187.
16. Ibid.
17. Ibid.
18. Susan Stryker, "Sex and Death among the Cyborgs: Interview with Allucquere Stone," *Wired*, May 1996, 136.
19. Ibid.
20. Erik Davis, "Technopagans," *Wired*, July 1995, 176.
21. Timothy Leary and Eric Gullicsen, "High-tech Paganism-Digital Polytheism," no date, Timothy Leary home page, at: http://www.leary.com.
22. Ibid.
23. On the New Age movement, see Douglas Groothuis, *Unmasking the New Age: Is There a New Religious Movement Trying to Transform Society?* (Downers Grove, IL: InterVarsity Press, 1986), *Confronting the New Age* (Downers Grove, IL: InterVarsity Press, 1988), and *Jesus in an Age of Controversy* (Eugene, OR: Harvest House, 1996).
24. See Jeff Zaleski, "Cyberspirit," *Yoga Journal*, March/April 1996, 69.
25. For more on Teilhard, see Tal Brooke, "Preparing for the Cosmic Millennium and the Coming Global Church," *Spiritual Counterfeits Project Journal* 19, nos. 2–3 (1995): 4–17.
26. This is argued in a favorable article by John R. Mabry, "Cyberspace and the Dream of Teilhard De Chardin," *Creation Spirituality*, Summer 1994, 25.
27. Quoted in Spencer Reiss, "Is He the Net's Thomas Jefferson? John Perry Barlow on Tour," *Yahoo! Internet Life*, July/August 1996, 113.

28. Gary Wolf, "The Wisdom of Saint Marshall, the Holy Fool," *Wired*, January 1996, 125.
29. Matie Molinaro, Corrine McLuhan, William Toye, eds. *Letters of Marshall McLuhan* (New York: Oxford University Press, 1987), 370.
30. Hillary Clinton, for one, is reported to have consulted Houston. See Sonya Ross, "Hillary Clinton's Spirited Discussions," *Rocky Mountain News* 24 June 1996, 2A. For a hilarious commentary on Jean Houston's published viewpoints, see John Leo, "Exclusive!! Jean Houston Speaks," *U.S. News & World Report*, 8 July 1996, 23.
31. David Jay Brown and Rebecca McClen Novick, "Forging the Possible Human with Jean Houston," *Voices From the Edge*, eds. David Jay Brown and Rebecca McClen Novick (Freedom, CA: The Freedom Press, 1995), 246.
32. For more on shamanism, see Groothuis, *Unmasking*, 137; and Groothuis, *Jesus*, 242–43.
33. Alexander Star, "Oliver Stone's Cyberkitsch," *New Republic*, 6/14/93; online documentation.
34. Davis, "Technopagans," 174.
35. Ibid., 128.
36. Ibid.
37. Ibid.
38. Ibid.
39. Ibid., 131.
40. Indra's net and its relationship to claims in New Age scientific thought is analyzed in Groothuis, *Unmasking*, 98–109.
41. Sven Birkerts, "Homo Virtualis," in *Dumbing Down: Essays on the Stripmining of American Culture*, eds. Katharine Washburn and John Thornton (New York: Norton, 1996), 211.
42. Davis, "Technopagans," 180.
43. Ibid., 178.
44. Ibid.
45. Ibid.
46. On this theme, see Douglas Groothuis, *Christianity That Counts: Being a Christian in a Non-Christian World* (Grand Rapids, MI: Baker Books, 1994), 102–5.
47. Michael Heim, *The Metaphysics of Virtual Reality* (New York: Oxford University Press, 1994), 85.
48. Abraham Heschel, *Man Is not Alone: A Philosophy of Religion* (New York: Farrar, Straus, and Giroux, Inc., 1951), 33–34.
49. Blaise Pascal, *Pensées*, trans. A. J. Krailsheimer (New York: Penguin, 1966), 407/465, p. 147.
50. Mark 7:21–22.
51. Pascal, 149/430, p. 77.
52. Ibid., 149/430, p. 78.
53. Hebrews 1:3; 4:13.

54. Colossians 1:27.
55. Isaiah 57:15.
56. See Rousas John Rushdoony, "Power From Below," *The Journal of Christian Reconstruction* 1, no. 2 (Winter 1974), 7–10. On the dynamics of magic in relation to Gnosticism, see Carl Raschke, *The Interruption of Eternity: Modern Gnosticism and the Origins of the New Religious Consciousness* (Chicago: Nelson-Hall, 1980), 30–32.
57. See Deuteronomy 18:10–12.
58. "The Counterfeit Infinity" is a chapter title from Os Guinness, *The Dust of Death: The Sixties Counterculture and How it Changed America Forever* (Wheaton, IL: Crossway Books, 1994), 235–74. This chapter on hallucinogenic drugs is highly recommended.
59. 2 Corinthians 11:14.
60. John 8:44.
61. On the dangers of occult involvement, see Douglas Groothuis, *Confronting the New Age* (Downers Grove, IL: InterVarsity Press, 1988), 76–83.
62. Rushkoff, *Cyberia*, 148–49.
63. See chapter five on the correspondence view of truth.
64. I owe this example to Winfried Corduan, *Reasonable Faith* (Nashville, TN: Broadman & Holman, 1993), 60–61.
65. See R. C. Sproul, *Not a Chance: The Myth of Chance in Modern Science and Cosmology* (Grand Rapids, MI: Baker Books, 1994), 92–93, and Guinness, 238.
66. 1 Timothy 2:5–6, NRSV.
67. Tal Brooke, "Cyberspace: Storming Digital Heaven," *SCP Journal* 19:4-20:1 (1995): 16.
68. Titus 1:15–16.
69. Rushkoff, *Cyberia*, 205.
70. Ibid.
71. Ibid., 144.
72. Ibid., 198.
73. Ibid., ix.
74. See Francis A. Schaeffer, *The God Who is There: Speaking Historic Christianity into the Twentieth Century* (Downers Grove, IL: InterVarsity Press, 1976), 56–62.
75. Matthew 23:27.
76. Quoted in Zaleski, 72.
77. Psalm 127:1.
78. Matthew 7:24–27.

Chapter 8: Exploring Virtual Community

1. Richard Mouw, *Uncommon Decency: Christian Civility in an Uncivil World* (Downers Grove, IL: InterVarsity Press, 1992), 12.

2. John Marks, "The American Uncivil Wars," U.S. News & World Report, 22 April 1996, 68–72.
3. John Leo, "Foul Words, Foul Culture," U.S. News & World Report, April 11, 1996, 73.
4. Ibid.
5. Os Guinness, The American Hour (New York: Free Press, 1992).
6. See Charles Sykes, A Nation of Victims (New York: St. Martin's Press, 1992).
7. Psalm 133:1, NRSV.
8. On this, see Faith Popcorn and Lys Marigold, Clicking: 16 Trends to Future Fit Your Life, Your Work, and Your Business (New York: HarperCollins, 1996), 51–63.
9. For some insightful comments on the significance of the Walkman, see Jacques Ellul, The Technological Bluff (Grand Rapids, MI: Eerdmans, 1990), 378.
10. Edward Cornish, "The Cyber Future," The Futurist, January–February 1996, special section, 4.
11. Ibid., 5.
12. Jan Clenski, "Computer-head Student Shares His World View," Rocky Mountain News, 10 January 1996, 31A.
13. Ibid.
14. Ibid.
15. Amitai Etzioni, The Spirit of Community (New York: Simon and Schuster, 1993), 260.
16. Richard John Neuhaus, "The Christian and the Church," in Transforming Our World: A Call to Action, ed. James M. Boice (Portland, OR: Multnomah Press, 1988), 120.
17. Quoted in the Daily Telegraph, London, 14 December 1988; cited in The Columbia Dictionary of Quotations (Columbia University Press, 1993), CD-ROM version.
18. William J. Mitchell, City of Bits: Place, Space, and the Infoban (Cambridge, MA: MIT Press, 1995), 166; see also 128–131.
19. David Wells, God in the Wasteland (Grand Rapids, MI: Eerdmans, 1994), 48.
20. Stephen L. Talbot, The Future Does not Compute: Transcending the Machines in Our Midst (Sebastopol, CA: O'Reilly and Associates, 1995), 107.
21. Ibid., 113.
22. Gregory Stock, Metaman: The Merging of Humans and Machines into a Global Superorganism (New York: Simon and Schuster, 1993), 204; quoted in Mark Slouka, War of the Worlds: Cyberspace and the High-Tech Assault on Reality (New York: Basic Books, 1995), 79.
23. Bill Gates with Nathan Myhvold and Peer Rinearson, The Road Ahead (New York: Viking, 1995), 92.

24. "On Line," *The Chronicle of Higher Education*, 21 June, 1996, A 17. The report cites the findings of the Georgia Institute of Technology's Graphic, Visualization & Usability Center.
25. Cited in Reginald Stuart, "High-Tech Redlining," *Utne Reader*, March-April 1995, 73; originally published in *Emerge*, November 1994.
26. On this see, Sunteel Raton, "A New Divide Between Haves and Have-Nots?" *Time*, Special Issue: Welcome to Cyberspace, Spring 1995, 25–26.
27. Clifford Stoll, *Silicon Snake Oil: Second Thoughts on the Information Highway* (New York: Doubleday, 1995), 60.
28. Ibid., 62.
29. Slouka, 54.
30. Clay Shirky, *Voices From the Net* (Emeryville, CA: Ziff-Davis Press, 1995), 42.
31. Peter Drucker, *The Effective Executive* (New York: HarperBusiness, 1966), 67.
32. Ibid., 68.
33. Daryl Fogal, "Real Fake," Interview with Martin Hash, *Wired*, June 1996, 157.
34. Marshall McLuhan, *Understanding Media: The Extensions of Man* (New York: McGraw-Hill Book Company, 1964), 19.
35. 1 Corinthians 15:33; see also Psalm 1. Interestingly, McLuhan refers to "the Psalmist" in the above quotation. He was aware that the idea that "we become what we behold" was biblical.
36. Jeremy Rifkin, *Time Wars: The Primary Conflict in Human History* (New York: Simon and Schuster, 1987, 26. He is referring to the work of Craig Brod, *Technostress* (Reading, MA: Addison-Wesley, 1984).
37. Brod, 94.
38. John Seabrook, "My First Flame," *New Yorker*, 6 June 1994, 73–74.
39. Rifkin, 27.
40. Nicholas Negroponte, *Being Digital* (New York: Alfred A. Knopf, 1995), 191–92. It is interesting that Negroponte, high-tech guru that he is, uses the outmoded term "carriage return" when computers, unlike typewriters, have no carriages that return at all. Instead, they have "enter" keys.

Chapter 9: Virtual Community: Trust, Deception, and Infection

1. Francis Fukuyama, *Trust: The Social Virtues and the Creation of Prosperity* (New York: Free Press, 1995), 25.
2. Ibid., 26.
3. Cited in John Seabrook, "My First Flame," *New Yorker*, 6 June 1994, 72; emphasis added.
4. Cited in Bob King, "Web of Deceit," *Internet Underground*, June 1996, 26.
5. Ibid., 28.
6. Ibid., 29.
7. Ibid., 28.

8. Ibid., 29.
9. See Robert Wright, "The Cybersmear," *Time*, 8 July 1996, 46.
10. Daryll Fogal, "Real Fake," Interview with Martin Hash, *Wired*, 157.
11. See Clifford Stoll, *Silicon Snake Oil* (New York: Doubleday, 1995), 84.
12. William J. Mitchell, "When Is Seeing Believing?" *Scientific American*, February 1994, 70.
13. Ibid.
14. Ibid., 73.
15. Randall Lane, "The Magician," *Forbes*, 11 March 1996, 124.
16. Ibid., 124.
17. See Paula Parisi, "The New Hollywood Silicon Stars," *Wired*, December 1995, 142ff.
18. Sherry Turkle, *Life on the Screen: Identity in an Age of Internet* (New York: Simon and Schuster, 1995), 88.
19. Ibid., 90–93.
20. Michael McCormick, "Invasion of the Internet Impostors," *Internet Underground*, July 1996, 40.
21. Ibid., 39.
22. Ibid.
23. Ibid., 40.
24. Ibid., 37.
25. Edward Cornish, "The Cyber Future," *The Futurist*, January–February 1996, special section, 7.
26. I owe this insight to Rebecca Merrill Groothuis.
27. Bill Gates with Nathan Myhrvold and Peter Rinearson, *The Road Ahead* (New York: Viking, 1995), 79.
28. John Whalen, "Super Searcher," Interview with Reva Basch, *Wired*, May 1995, 153.
29. James Fallows, "Computers: The Java Theory," *Atlantic Monthly*, March 1996, 116.
30. Clifford Stoll, *Silicon Snake Oil: Second Thoughts on the Information Highway* (New York: Doubleday, 1995), 197.
31. Gates, et al, 157–83.
32. Gary Chapman, "Friction-Free Economy? No Jobs. Aye, There's the Rub," *San Jose Mercury News*, 15 January 1996; Business Monday section; online documentation. On the effects of technological change on unemployment, see Jeremy Rifkin, *The End of Work: The Decline of the Global Labor Force and the Dawn of the Post-Market Era* (New York: G. P. Putman and Sons, 1995). Rifkin's descriptions and concerns are far more sane than his recommendations for future policies.
33. Nicholas Negroponte, *Being Digital* (New York: Alfred A. Knopf, 1995), 102.
34. See Stoll, 95.
35. Negroponte, 235.

36. Jean Baudrillard, *The Transparency of Evil*, trans. James Benedict (New York: Verso, 1993), 167; emphasis added. See also Jaron Lanier, "My Problem with Agents," *Wired*, November 1996, 157–58.

37. There is, however, little about the "global" village that resembles a geographical village. See Stephen L. Talbot, *The Future Does Not Compute: Transcending the Machines in our Midst* (Sebastopol, CA: O'Reilly and Associates, 1995), 105–13.

38. Seabrook, 73.

39. See Winn Schwartau, *Information Warfare: Chaos on the Electronic Superhighway* (New York; Thunder's Mouth Press, 1995), 107.

40. Ibid., 17.

41. Ibid.

42. Douglas Rushkoff, *Media Virus: Hidden Agendas in Popular Culture*, revised edition (New York: Ballantine Books, 1996).

43. Nathaniel Sheppard Jr., "Hate in Cyberspace," *Emerge*, July 1996, 36.

44. Ibid., 38

45. Ibid., 36.

46. Ibid.

47. Michelle Slatalla, "Who Can I Turn To?" *Wired*, May 1996, 119.

48. Ibid.

Chapter 10: Online Christianity?

1. See 2 Timothy 2:15.

2. Mark Noll, *The Scandal of the Evangelical Mind* (Grand Rapids, MI: William B. Eerdmans, 1994), 127.

3. I am not aware of how sophisticated the programs are in this area, but this kind of temptation should be avoided at every level of technology.

4. Derrick de Kerkhove, *The Skin of Culture: Investigating the New Electronic Technology: Tool, Toy or Tyrant* (Toronto: Somerville House Publishing, 1995), 62; quoted in Donald L. Baker, "Welcome to the CyberMillenium: Part One: Hidden Building Blocks of the City of Bits," *SCP Journal* 19:4-20:1 (1995): 24.

5. Blaise Pascal, *Pensées*, trans. A. J. Krailsheimer (New York: Penguin, 1966), 651/369, p. 240.

6. See all of Psalm 119 on the wisdom of meditating on God's word.

7. Cited by Charles Colson, "Apologetics for the Church: Why Christians Are Losing the Culture War," *Christian Research Journal*, Summer 1996, 52.

8. See Douglas Groothuis, "Telling the Truth Today," *Focal Point*, Spring 1995, 3–4; and David Wells, *No Place for Truth or Whatever Happened to Evangelical Theology?* (Grand Rapids, MI: William B. Eerdmans, 1993).

9. Acts 17:11.

10. Revelation 3:17.

11. Langdon Winner, "Three Paradoxes of the Information Age," in *Culture on the Brink: Ideologies of Technology*, ed. Gretchen Bender and Timothy Druckery (Seattle, WA: Bay Press, 1994), 192.

12. Ibid.

13. Neil Postman, *Technopoly*, (New York, Alfred A. Knopf, 1992), 115.

14. Eric Pement, "Witnessing Through Computer Bulletin Boards," *Christian Research Journal*, Spring/Summer 1994, 7. On netiquitte, see also Baker, *Christian Cyberspace Companion*, 112–16.

15. Pement, 7.

16. E. Stanley Jones, *Christ at the Round Table* (New York: Grosset and Dunlap Publishers, 1928), 15

17. See Theodore Roszak, *The Cult of Information: A Neo-Luddite Treatise on High-Tech, Artificial Intelligence, and the True Art of Thinking*, revised edition (Berkeley, CA: University of California Press, 1994), 58–9.

18. See Allucquere Rosanne Stone, *The War of Desire and Technology at the Close of the Mechanical Age* (Cambridge, MA: The MIT Press, 1995), 10–11. Stone's discussion of the character of interactivity is insightful, but it is not clear if she thinks true interactivity is limited to human-to-human interaction.

19. Romans 1:11–12.

Conclusion: Eloquent Realities

1. See Jerry Mander, *In the Absence of the Sacred: The Failure of Technology and the Survival of the Indian Nations* (San Francisco: Sierra Club Books, 1991), 50. I am not as negative as is Mander, nor do I embrace his overall worldview.

2. See Kirkpatrick Sale, *Rebels Against the Future: The Luddites and Their War on the Industrial Revolution: Lessons for the Computer Age* (Reading, MA: Addison Wesley, 1995). For a critical review challenging much of Kirkpatrick's understanding of history, see Steven Marcus, "Rage Against the Machine," *New Republic*, 10 June 1996, 30–38.

3. See Theodore Roszak, *The Cult of Information: A Neo-Luddite Treatise on High-Tech, Artificial Intelligence, and the True Art of Thinking*, second edition (Berkeley, CA: University of California Press, 1994), xvii–xviii.

4. Neil Postman, *Technopoly: The Surrender of Culture to Technology* (New York: Alfred A. Knopf, 1992), 184.

5. I owe the insight of this paragraph to Rebecca Merrill Groothuis.

6. Mark Dery, *Escape Velocity: Cyberculture at the End of the Century* (New York: Grove Press, 1996, 254-55). Dery is citing Joseph Campbell with Bill Moyers, *The Power of Myth* (New York: Doubleday, 1988), 211.

7. For a critique of Campbell's worldview, see Douglas Groothuis, *Christianity that Counts: Being a Christian in a Non-Christian World* (Grand Rapids, MI: Baker Books, 1994), 150–62.

8. On this problem, see R. C. Zaehner, *Our Savage God: The Perverse Use of Eastern Thought* (New York: Sheed and Ward, 1974); David K. Clark and Norman L. Geisler, *Apologetics in the New Age: A Christian Critique of Pantheism* (Grand Rapids, MI: Baker Books, 1990), 203–21; Douglas R. Groothuis, *Unmasking the New Age* (Downers Grove, IL: InterVarsity Press, 1986), 152–55.

9. See Mark Slouka, *War of the Worlds: Cyberspace and the High-Tech Assault on Reality* (New York: Basic Books, 1995), 134–42. On the ethical problems of naturalism see James W. Sire, *The Universe Next Door*, second edition (Downers Grove, IL: InterVarsity Press, 1988), 98-103; and J.P. Moreland, *Scaling the Secular City* (Grand Rapids, MI: Baker Books, 1987), 105–32.

10. Postman, 92–106.

11. Dennis Oliver, "The Virtual Church," *Areopagus*, Pentecost 1995, 28.

12. Wendell Berry, *What Are People For? Essays By Wendell Berry* (New York: North Point Press, 1990), 172.

13. Albert Borgmann, *Crossing the Postmodern Divide* (Chicago: University of Chicago Press, 1992), 108.

14. Max Picard, *The World of Silence*, trans. Stanley Godman (Chicago: Henry Regnery Company, 1952), 57.

15. See Genesis 11:1–9.

16. I owe this paragraph to Rebecca Merrill Groothuis.

17. Picard, 57.

18. Ecclesiastes 5:2–3.

19. Matthew 12:37.

20. See Thomas Cahill, *How the Irish Saved Civilization: The Untold Story of Ireland's Heroic Role from the Fall of Rome to the Rise of Medieval Europe* (New York: Doubleday, 1995).

21. Quoted by Daniel J. Boorstin, *Cleopatra's Nose: Essays on the Unexpected* (New York: Vintage Books, 1994), 173.

22. Clifford Stoll, *Silicon Snake Oil: Second Thoughts on the Information Superhighway* (New York: Doubleday, 1995), 138.

23. Borgmann, 119. I have supplied several of my own examples for his essential concept.

24. Cited in Jack Kisling, "How Much Control is Enough?" *Denver Post*, 20 July 1995.

25. Psalm 19:1.

26. See Romans 1:19–20.

27. Psalm 139:14.

28. C. S. Lewis, *The Weight of Glory and Other Addresses*, revised and expanded edition, ed. Walter Hooper (New York: Macmillan, 1980), 18–19.

BIBLIOGRAPHY

Baker, Jason. *Christian Cyberspace Companion*. Grand Rapids, MI: Baker Book House, 1995. A helpful, practical guide to understanding the nature and functions of cyberspace.

Baudrillard, Jean. Trans. James Benedict. *The Transparency of Evil: Essays on Extreme Phenomena*. New York: Verso, 1990. Contains often enigmatic but sometimes insightful reflections on the nature and impact of information technologies.

Birkerts, Sven. *The Gutenberg Elegies: The Fate of Reading in an Electronic Age*. New York: Faber and Faber, 1994. A generally Luddite critique but full of fascinating and important observations. Flirts with a Christian worldview, but fails to embrace it.

Borgman, Albert. *Crossing the Postmodern Divide*. Chicago: The University of Chicago Press, 1992. A philosophical reflection on the nature of postmodernity in relation to modern technologies. Hints at a theistic worldview in places.

Dery, Mark. *Escape Velocity: Cyberculture at the End of the Century*. New York: Grove Press, 1996. An indepth, critical look at the cultural implications of a variety of new technologies, including cyberspace applications. Suggests a pantheistic worldview and is hostile to Christianity.

Ellul, Jacques. *The Technological Bluff*. Grand Rapids, MI: Wm. B. Eerdmans Publishing Company, 1990. A broad-ranging discussion of a variety of technologies, including computer communication.

Gates, Bill with Nathan Myhrvold and Peter Rinearson. *The Road Ahead*. New York: Viking Penguin, 1995. A digitopian history and scenario of computing that is largely oblivious to the deleterious effects of the technologies it glorifies.

Groothuis, Douglas. *Confronting the New Age*. Downers Grove, IL: InterVarsity Press, 1988. Although it does not address cyberspace, it critiques the worldview of pantheistic monism that animates technoshamanism.

Heim, Mark. *The Metaphysics of Virtual Reality*. New York: Oxford University Press, 1993. A collection of essays on the nature and cultural impact of computer technologies. Influenced by Taoism and Heidegger.

McLuhan, Marshall. *Understanding Media: The Extensions of Man*. New York: McGraw-Hill, 1964. Pivotal book that made the sociology of electronic media a discipline in and of itself.

Negroponte, Nicholas. *Being Digital*. New York: Alfred A. Knopf. A digitopian view of the transition to a fully digitized society, written by a leader in these technologies.

Pascal, Blaise. *Pensées*. Trans. A. J. Krailsheimer. New York: Penguin Books, 1966. A collection of fragments defending Christianity, which often relate to the human tendency to distract oneself from matters of ultimate concern. Very applicable to many cyberspace technologies.

Picard, Max. *The World of Silence*. Trans. Stanley Godman. Chicago: Henry Regnery Company, 1961. Neglected classic on the modern technological assault on silence.

Postman, Neil, *Technopoly: The Surrender of Culture to Technology*. New York: Alfred A. Knopf, 1992. A penetrating critique of the dynamics of modern technologies that is sympathetic toward religious traditions without embracing any of them.

Rushkoff, Douglas. *Cyberia: Life in the Trenches of Hyperspace*. San Francisco: HarperSanFrancisco, 1995. A disturbing, sympathetic analysis of the dark underbelly of cyberculture by a leading Generation X social critic.

Roszak, Theodore. *The Cult of Information: A Neo-Luddite Treatise on High Tech, Artificial Intelligence and the True Art of Thinking*. Second Edition. Berkeley, CA: University of California Press, 1994. A discerning critique that attempts to conserve the human dimension of culture and knowledge. Roszak's pantheistic worldview does not intrude overly upon his analysis.

Slouka, Mark. *War of the Worlds: Cyberspace and the High-Tech Assault on Reality*. New York: HarperCollins, 1995. A brief but often cogent complaint against the depersonalizing aspects of cyberspace written from a naturalistic perspective critical of Christianity.

Stoll, Clifford. *Silicon Snake Oil: Second Thoughts on the Information Highway*. New York: Doubleday, 1995. An informal but well-informed romp through the downside of cyberspace, written by a computer expert. Often humorous.

Talbot, Stephen L. *The Future Does Not Compute: Transcending the Machines in Our Midst*. Sebastopal, CA: O'Reilly and Associates, 1995. A large, somewhat verbose treatment that is often perceptive in its concerns about the dehumanizing aspects of computer technologies. Written by a computer expert who is an Anthroposophist (follower of the pantheistic mystic Rudolf Steiner).

Toffler, Alvin and Heidi. *Creating a New Civilization: The Politics of the Third Wave*. Atlanta: Turner Publishing, Inc., 1995. A brief digitopian tract, full of hype and unguarded overstatements about the much-vaunted "information age."

Turkle, Sherry. *Life on the Screen: Identity in the Age of the Internet*. New York: Simon and Schuster, 1995. An interpretation favorable toward cyberspace because of its tendencies to reinforce postmodernist themes.

Woolley, Benjamin. *Virtual Worlds: A Journey in Hype and Hyperreality*. New York: Penguin Books, 1993. A careful, witty, and critical investigation.

Since receiving his Ph.D. in philosophy from the University of Oregon in 1993, Douglas Groothuis has served as assistant professor of philosophy of religion and ethics at Denver Seminary. He has been a visiting instructor at New College-Berkeley, Seattle Pacific University, the University of Oregon, and Westminster Theological Seminary West.

He served in campus ministry for twelve years at two universities and continues to give lectures and debates on college campuses. He is also a frequent guest on many local and national radio programs.

He has written for a number of popular and scholarly publications, and has authored seven books, including *Deceived by the Light* and *Jesus in an Age of Controversy.*

He is married to author and editor Rebecca Merrill Groothuis.

He and his wife can be reached at their Web page at: http://www.gospelcom.net/ivpress/groothuis. His e-mail address is: DGROOTH133@aol.com.